COMING TO YOUR
SENSES

BETH JOHNSON

D1411555

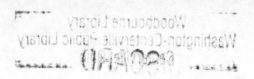

ISBN-10: 1480210668
EAN-13: 9781480210660

Library of Congress Control Number: 2012920516
CreateSpace Independent Publishing Platform North Charleston,
South Carolina

Printed in the United States of America.

Feel
See
Smell
Taste
Hear

When we utilize our five senses,
we develop our sixth.

TABLE OF CONTENTS

ACKNOWLEDGMENTS

Writing *Coming to Your Senses* was a two-man show. I wrote my little heart out, and then my good friend Cheryl Williams came to my aid and made the sentences shine and pass the English muster. Cheryl Williams is a dream friend and my senior editor, but those tag lines fall short in giving her enough credit. She is a voracious reader, punctuating fool, sharp as they come, and no misspelled words pass her fingers. These are all good talents to have in an editor, but the quality she possesses that I cherish the most and made the book so much easier to write is her sense of humor. Oh, how we love to laugh.

The hours that we spent on this book flew by. That she knows and lives my work made child's play out of what could have been a tedious endeavor. Having been involved with Inner Vision Meditation since its beginning, it helped her to help me create perfect sentences with which to project the honesty and purity of the process. It has been so much fun working together, and I know she will be asking me about doing another book just as soon as this one leaves her hands.

I am good with that. I may write one someday about how amazing she is. God bless good friends.

Thanks again, BBB,

From your BBB

I must acknowledge one other. No one can write a book if her partner or husband is not on board with the project. I am so fortunate to have a wonderful husband who supports my efforts 99 percent of the time. That other 1 percent, he complains about having to look at the back of my head while I am miles away, engrossed in trying to capture the right phraseology for a sentence. I can't say that I blame him, because it does take a lot of solo time, but he has been so patient! And, as an enormous bonus, he gets this wonderful gleam of pride in his eyes when I talk about what I have accomplished that day.

My mother was the first one to point out that precious look he gets when he is proud of me. I think of her when I see it and know that she is seeing it, too. Sometimes I feel she has joined him in his gaze and I can feel her presence peeking through. It makes me cry tears of joy and makes me want to keep writing.

I love you, Bruce, and I know you can feel it.

And Mom, what can I say? You showed me how to love by loving me.

COMING TO YOUR SENSES

*O*ur group follows her to the meditation temple. Slowly, silently we walk. She enters first and gently shuts the door while we wait just outside. The wait passes quickly as we busy ourselves taking off our shoes to be ready to enter. Our eyes meet and speak volumes, but we don't talk...we just don't. We just wait. As the wait grows a little longer than I expected, I think to myself how we all have such trust in this woman. The thought makes me smile, because the lessons are always different and I wonder what might be in store for us today.

The door begins to open...she greets each one of us with a nod of Namaste and gestures for us to take our seats. The look in her eye is different. What was it, more resolute, more...? But before I can give it much thought she is passing out blindfolds for each of us. Now that is odd...we meditate with our eyes closed anyway. I wonder why the masks are needed, but I do not question. I put on my mask and there is nothing but silence. A good kind of silence, but I can feel it. It makes the anticipation of what is to come even stronger.

Then she says a single word: Listen. She said it with clarity, certainty, and as a command.

Again silence. I thought we were to listen to the silence. And then it came. One solid beat of a drum. The resonance in the temple was incredible.

Then she says it again: Listen. But this time the word sounds like an invitation to join the drum.

The beat of the drum becomes rhythmic and the vibrations fill the room. Her next words are, "Let yourself see the vibrations."

I am very aware of feeling the vibrations, but never had I thought to try to see them.

"Let your imagination take you to the place where you can see everything you feel. Let your inner eye see what your body can sense."

I am beginning to get the sense of what she is asking us to do when the sound of a Tibetan bowl takes the place of the drumbeat. The dramatic switch in the tone makes an impression on my body and I can see/feel the change. I can see the vibrations.

Then silence again.

And then another command comes: Feel.

She is placing something in my hand—a piece of fabric. I am thinking, "It is so soft," when she says, "See inside you…see and feel the sensations of your body related to the study of what you are holding."

I think, "How do I do that?" As if she can hear my thoughts, she says, "Feel each sensation in your body as a vibration, and observe them."

She places another piece of fabric in my hand. This time it is coarse like burlap; I'm trying to figure out if that was what it is when she says, "Don't think…just feel and see where in your body you react to the differences in touch." I move away from the thought and go in search of the sensations in my body; I find them and observe them. My thoughts creep in for a second and begin to judge, and again it's like she is listening to my thoughts. "Allow any and all to be just as it is."

There is silence again, and this time I am settled in my own world.

Another instructional word comes: Taste.

A small cup is placed in my hand and I am told to take a sip.

She says softly to all of us, "Do not try to discern what the taste is. Feel the taste in your body and go to those sensations."

I know how to do this now and when I taste what I know to be cranberry juice, the sensations in my mouth go wild. I see them and I see the reaction of the rest of my body as well.

Another cup comes and the instructions are the same. "Feel the sensations of the body as it receives the liquid." This time it is water and there is a pervasive, gentle soothing sensation that covers my entire body…even down to my toes.

The silence that follows is luxurious. I could not feel more in love with time.

Then I hear the soft word: Smell.

An aroma from heaven is passed beneath my nose. The explosion of sensations is so intense I gasp. My body seems to shoot upward. Higher and higher I go. I can still hear her voice in the background saying, "Let all be. See it all. Feel it all." And that is exactly what I was doing. I was enveloped in my own bodily sensations…alive and exhilarated. I was an angel with wings.

Time passes, but I have no idea how long. There is nothing but bliss upon bliss as my body leads the way with its wondrous sensations.

Then I heard her speak again. Softly but clearly spoken she said, "Now remove your blindfolds and see."

I was not sure I could move, but slowly I maneuvered the cover from my eyes. And then she says, as if one letter at a time, "Feel what you see."

As I look at my friends, I feel them. I could feel we were all blended together in the seamless flow of life. I can't tell you how profoundly that hit me.

We all sit and drink each other in.

The room is spellbound by sensations. It is euphoric and yet very real.

We do nothing but sit and feel the interaction of each other's presence.

In silence and in awe, we relish our new understanding of our bodies and our senses. We have awakened them, we are honoring them, and they are flourishing. We have come to our senses.

Present in the SilentPlace Temple were:

Jill Anderson, Susan Carter, Trish Cayce, Debbie Haggard, Karen Kott, Lynda Richardson, Shari Scott, and Cheryl Williams.

INTRODUCTION

By oneself the evil is done, and it is one's self
who suffers;
By oneself the evil is not done, and by one's
self one becomes pure.
The pure and the impure come from oneself:
no man can purify another.
— The Dhammapada

This book is about you. It is not your conventional New Age self-help book. It is a book about gaining new insights and developing a stronger and clearer understanding of your true nature. There is nothing unique about the intent of this book, but the methodology and usefulness of its content places it in a category all its own.

Imagine being able to transform old attitudes, trapped fears, or redundant useless mind dialogue into pure creativity. I want to show you that you can understand, and physically sense, what stands in your way of feeling connected to your higher power. With me guiding you and encouraging you to look deeply into your inner core, you will have the opportunity to open your eyes to see and tune your ears to listen to your own inner wisdom. That inner wisdom, that inner knowing, is your life-guide. It is your sixth sense.

Like an alchemist, you will learn how to spin your old habits and misconceptions into the golden truth of you. Nothing will be lost, but nothing will be the same. The old is transformed into the new. Through our discussions, you will see through to your purest self. You will be releasing the timeworn, useless, habit-driven belief system that you have clung to and in so doing make the way for fresh new energizing concepts. You will create a new, truth-based perspective on your entire life. You will learn when faced with life challenges that there comes a time to stop the process of thinking and begin employing your sensory skills. Your senses will lead you into a meditation I call Inner Vision Meditation. There you will find the authentic, Soul-connected sacredness of you. There you will find your answers.

CHAPTER 1

MEDITATION HAS EVOLVED INTO MORE THAN QUIETING THE MIND

If you are not familiar with meditation, you may have myriad ideas about what it is or what it is not. And if you *are* familiar with meditation, you could still have myriad ideas about what it is and what it is not.

There are numerous methods of meditation, and although the various practices retain somewhat the same goal, they vary greatly in style and technique. I have been a meditator for the past twentyish years and have tried some form of most, if not all, of them. While exploring the different techniques along the way I came to (or did it come to me?) a wonderfully simple method of meditation.

Interest in meditation has increased over the years, but as mentioned earlier, the basic intent has remained the same for the eons it has been around—meditation is for quieting the mind. It really is left up to one's imagination as to what might happen after accomplishing the seemingly next-to-impossible task of zipping the lips of the inner voice in your head.

Even though the practice of meditation can be challenging, it has proven throughout the ages to be successful in helping people to relax, relieve stress, and in general increase their quality of life. I believe all meditation practices, no matter what the style, can be beneficial to you, your body, and your life.

But (and, yes, there is a "but") I have come upon an approach to meditation that stands apart from all the others. It goes way beyond mollifying a hard day at the office or a sleepless night with a newborn baby. This technique expands the whole scope of meditation. The task of emptying your mind of thoughts is no longer difficult, and once the thoughts are gone, so is the unwanted clutter in your head and body. And that is just the beginning of what this new method presents to you. It gives you tools or spiritual implements to reveal, discover, and recognize your own inner truth. It gives you a way to learn from your own inner wisdom, your Higher Power, your sixth sense.

To see how Inner Vision Meditation differs from the others, I will give you a brief description of a number of the more familiar practices.

Transcendental Meditation is one of the better-known methods. A mantra (such as a symbolic word, sound, or phrase) is repeated silently to narrow the conscious awareness and eliminate all thoughts from the mind. The act of focusing exclusively on the mantra helps achieve a state of perfect stillness and consciousness.

Mindfulness Meditation is as the name suggests. The meditator is to be mindful of everything, and in so doing, increase awareness of the present moment. Attention is focused on the flow of the breath and as thoughts appear, they are to be observed without judgment.

Then there is *Guided Meditation*, sometimes called guided imagery or visualization. In this method, mental images are selected that are found to be relaxing, such as a luscious green valley, a gentle stream, or simply a soothing color. Teachers or guides lead the way as they introduce these peaceful images. They might focus on one scene or create a mesmerizing journey, both designed to enable the listener to relax and release tension.

Lastly, there is another form that I call *Visual Mantra Meditation*. In this style a symbol, scene, or object is selected and zeroed in on. Whatever is chosen is focused upon with all one's might. When I visited a Buddhist monastery in Thailand, the monks used this method. They began by chanting and then moved into the meditation. They were then asked to visualize being in the "center of the center." The leader repeated, "Be in the center of the center," every ten minutes or so. The intent here was to focus on going deeper inward and in so doing, the mind was to become silent.

In several of these styles, the technique of visualizing is used in order to captivate thoughts and emotions. Inner Vision Meditation also uses visualization, but the manner in which it introduces the images to the meditation is one of the distinctive and unique features of this new approach.

In *Inner Vision Meditation* the object to be envisioned is revealed to you through your own intuitive senses. When you enter the meditation, you have no preconceived ideas of what you are going to find and this frees you from all expectations. Teaching you to attune yourself to your senses is my intent. Your senses are not what need the work——it is your ability to let them do their job that is the task at hand.

In order to do this, it is helpful for you when reading this book to give yourself the freedom of thinking differently. I will discuss things that you have most likely never given any thought to. I will introduce ideas that may seem strange, counter to your current beliefs, or just downright odd. If you let the story develop, it will fall into place and you will be glad you hung in there.

CHAPTER 2

DISPELLING THE MYTH
THAT THE ABILITY TO THINK
IS YOUR MOST VALUABLE TOOL

If meditation is thought to be the practice of quieting the mind, what exactly is meditation silencing? Is it your highly revered thinking?

Isn't humankind's ability to think and reason what separates us from other species on Earth? If so, what is there to be gained by muffling the very thing that we hold in such high regard?

There are certainly circles of academia that would resist any thought of giving up even a moment of their ability to think. If they believe that thinking is humankind's most valuable tool and those who practice traditional meditation are trying to stifle it, it is possible the two of them are not viewing the activity of thinking in the same vein. So what, exactly, is thinking?

What I have found is that most people believe thinking occurs when they are using their conscious mind to make rational decisions, to objectively evaluate, or to call something to mind, such as a phone number. All of these processes are where the conscious mind is engaged in a useful purpose.

So what about all the other thoughts that swim around in our heads? Are they considered to be thoughts and not classified as thinking?

Are we thinking when our mind engages in meaningless chatter as we gaze into space?

Or do we assign the word *thinking* only to our evaluation and assessment of that observation?

Do we consider the willy-nilly pondering of ideas as thinking?

Again, does thinking have to be productive to be deemed thinking?

I challenge that we honor elevated and productive thinking and we ignore or even disown all the rest.

To press this issue just a little further, decide if you believe it is your thinking that you call upon to be productive and creative. Or is it your ability to stay focused and be a good observer of yourself, others, and the world around you that spawns your ideas of creativity?

A good idea can seem to come out of nowhere. And once it has surfaced, that is when we begin to think. So we don't use our thinking to come up with good ideas—we use something much more powerful than thought.

Setting aside the act of thinking creates space for ideas to come forth and only then does thinking become useful, for then the mind can take what it has been given and cultivate it into reality. The mind then is the translator of a greater power from within. But we as humans have not fully comprehended this nifty little tidbit. We are unclear about what really goes on in our heads and which thoughts are worth keeping and what needs to be tossed.

Take daydreaming for instance: There are those who might consider daydreaming as a waste of time and a thought process we should keep to a minimum. I hold a very different view. Daydreaming is a healthy exercise in dissolving boundaries, and it sparks a far too stagnant imagination. It is also a productive way to seed our creative energy so that we can manifest that which we would like to have in our lives.

When we daydream, we are being very real with ourselves—so real that the thought of revealing those private thoughts and desires to others can feel threatening. If I were to guess why, I would say it is because we tell ourselves that no one would be interested in our personal fantasies and whims, but the real reason is that we don't want to look foolish or, worse yet, destroy our image or persona, so we keep most of our daydreaming secret.

The only thinking we would readily raise our hands to claim is our useful and productive thinking. That is the thinking that we all covet and the one that gets all the attention and good press. But "concrete thinking" or even "abstract thinking" only takes up a small portion of our heads' broadcast airtime. The rest is filled with a daydream every now and then, mindless chatter, and the *other* kind.

Yes, there is one other kind of thinking yet to be addressed. It is the voice of babble-on. The one that is quick to fill any and all the empty space that is not spoken for. This is where it gets tricky because you recognize this activity as being a voice in your head, but probably don't categorize it as thinking. If you subscribe to the idea that thinking is only acknowledged as such when it is productive, then this would not make the grade, for there is nothing productive about it.

I am speaking of the critical, challenging voice in your head.

The chatter from this tedious and imposing voice can become mind-numbing at times, and we are prone to ignore it. But the voice can be extremely captivating and convincing, especially when it takes on an argumentative, possibly competitive, or spiteful tone. When it is really revved up, the mind can go on an unbelievable and uncontrollable harangue. On these occasions, the filibustering usually has an agenda, which can range from being a tirade of self-deprecation to an unkind (to say the least) dialogue about someone else. Or, of course, we have all encountered the endless internal deliberation whose sole goal is to explain or justify our possibly inappropriate actions or our feelings toward an individual whom we feel has "done us wrong."

It is at these times that we find ourselves rehearsing scenario after scenario trying to rationalize or defend our position. There is no doubt these inner-mind dissertations have been stimulated by some intense emotional upheaval rooted in guilt or anger.

When left to its own devices, this kind of negatively energized thinking can become destructive, oppressive, and extremely unhealthy. If we do not acknowledge the existence of this type of thinking, or worse yet, if we try to handle its effects by fabricating a façade for pretending the thoughts do not exist, we will find ourselves being held captive by its imposing yet illusionary strength.

This repetitive thinking disguises itself as a necessary and important topic of discussion, but its true nature is more like a ruthless pirate who has the power to commandeer our mental faculties and hold them hostage until we come to our own rescue by "coming to our senses." If this menacing mind exercise is caught in the act, we can reestablish our position as captain of our thoughts; otherwise, we are in for an extended time of being controlled by our captor.

It is easy to see that this kind of thinking is not productive. This circular chatter has little or no effect on easing our stress level and has zero influence on alleviating any problems or resolving any disputes. This kind of thinking could more aptly be described as a dog chasing its tail. Where is the intelligence of our species in this form of thinking?

As intelligent as we are, we still fall for the myth that if we think about *it* more, analyze *it* more, dwell on *it* more; we can have an effect on *it*. If we don't think that our thinking is going to make a difference, why do we do it? We do it because we want to change the way we feel. We do it because we want relief. We are completely unaware that engaging in redundant thinking is not only unproductive, it is detrimental to our being able to gain the very thing we seek. What we are doing with our thoughts is having the exact opposite effect of what we want. The redundant dialogue blocks us from being able to experience anything other than the uncomfortable emotions we choose to keep reliving.

Without self-examination of thought, most people spend a good deal of their time in this type of thinking rather than in productive, creative thinking. Thinking things through is not as important as knowing when to be through with thinking.

If you are like so many people, you haven't given this much thought (a little humor here!), and may be wondering what possible difference all this talk about thinking can make anyway.

Once you are aware that not all thinking is equal, you can be more selective about your thoughts.

I will coach you in developing worthwhile skills for discerning the difference between useful thinking and thinking that is a waste of time and counterproductive.

CHAPTER 3

LEARNING TO FEEL THROUGH LIFE

If we have some inner thoughts that are not healthy to keep around in our heads, why do we? What is the antidote to those thoughts? The antidote is being able to feel. Seems simple enough, right? Well, it is simple in its original design, but we humans by natural evolution have moved our attention toward our intellect, and revel in our thought processes. In doing so we have lost touch with our ability to recognize the sensations of our core self. We think we are feeling when we are, in fact, experiencing the effects of a Starbucks latte, getting cranky from lack of sleep or food, or exhibiting the side effects of an antihistamine. We have lost the art of knowing that a bodily reaction generated by outside stimulants is not representative of our true selves. We have to find ways to move past the episodes we have labeled as "us" and into the more meaningful, meaty part of our self…the original piece of art we all have within.

I cannot count the number of people who have come to me to learn to meditate and say at the outset that they are quite certain they are a hopeless cause. They claim that the noise in their head is nonstop and it would be a miracle if it could stop for a second, much less for a full minute. I love it when I get someone like this because it is one more time I get to see that what I teach works.

All of us can succumb to episodes of brain babble, but it is also true that some people have a more driver-driver or Type A personality, which lends itself to an even greater propensity to excessive thought. The good news is that the Inner Vision Meditation method works just as well on all types of people. We start with something we all can do. We start by feeling and do so by using our five senses. Yes, our senses.

We sit and see, hear, taste, feel, and smell our way past the endless prattle of our minds. It is not necessary to employ all of the senses. Feel, hear, and see are readily handy, but if you do have time to add taste and smell to your ritual, you will be greatly rewarded. In this book I focus on touch/feeling, seeing, and hearing. Once any of these sensations captures your attention, the doorway is opened. The next step is one of choice. Do I follow this or do I choose to stay planted in my current thoughts?

If you choose to follow your body's sensations, you will find endless pearls of wisdom hidden within a headache or stiff neck. You might say to yourself, "That's no way to sell someone meditation," but if that is your Now, then that is where you begin.

It is easier to start in the Now and feel your way through to the moment of release than to dig in the past for the reasons of your pain.

CHAPTER 4

FINDING AND HONORING
YOUR SACREDNESS

The distance that you travel when you move from the thoughts of your mind to the sensations of your body cannot be measured. When you put yourself on your priority list and spend time observing the process, you can feel the distance you travel and welcome the sensation of entering the hometown of your inner self. This sensation of being welcomed home brings you to—maybe for the first time—the feeling of self-love. It has reduced many to tears. The feeling is both overwhelming and comforting, and it is there for you.

If that were not enough, one more extraordinary awakening lies in wait for you. It is yours alone, and has been with you before the beginning of time. I am speaking of your Soul. Yes, your Sacred Self, the place where you and your Creator are one. Feeling that connection is what this work is all about. When that centered power is tapped, you unleash untold creative potential. Your inner strength is set free and you feel the energy rejoicing as it moves freely along its natural path.

This may sound like a fairy tale but it's true, and I hope that you keep reading so you can share with others your experiences and let them know what gifts they have yet to open.

Learning to Turn Your Attention to Your Body

Learning to take time for yourself and pay attention to something as overlooked as your senses is your greatest hurdle.

A root desire must be stirred within. Everyone's outer-shell reasons for wanting to learn to mediate are different, but the root desire is the same. My task here is to touch upon something that will spark your interest and stir enough energy in you to ignite the flame of that root desire...your desire to be connected and at peace with your true God Self.

CHAPTER 5

TESTING THE WATERS

Whether you are in pursuit of a deep spiritual journey or seek a more balanced life, you must start with *you*.

"Your spiritual journey is as fruitful as you find yourself interesting."

This is a quote of mine, which I use to stir people's interest—interest in themselves. I want people to step out of their normal thoughts and take a moment for introspection. This statement always causes a momentary hush in the room. I have learned that the silence is created from them trying to sort out the meaning of my words. Since they likely expected something else to come out of my mouth, my statement throws them for a second. As they sort through the meaning of my words, it causes a boomerang effect. They fling their thoughts out into the ether in search of answers, but their thoughts return to themselves. It ends up back in their laps. When the meaning clicks, the shuffling of feet begins, followed by laughter…the kind of laughter generated from a feeling of awkwardness. It feels like I just took a peek inside their diaries.

So when you read the quote, examine your reaction. We are unaccustomed to putting ourselves in the limelight even if the recipient of the attention is me, myself, and I. The awkwardness we feel when asked to take a good, honest look inside ourselves is an example of the enormous disconnect between our outer world and our inner being.

When we distinguish our personal inner space as being different and separate from the outer world's activity, we make a quantum leap forward in understanding how life works. It is common to intertwine and entangle the two and subsequently lose sight of whom or what is the driving force of our lives. Contrary to what it may feel like at times, *you* and your God Self have the final say-so of how you will be affected by what transpires in your world. It is your ship, you are the captain, and you *alone* map your course.

All the things that you have mistakenly perceived as having control over you have gained that position of authority by you abdicating yours. Coming to that realization flips your life switch from the "off" position to the "on" position. It turns on the music of the Soul and transforms so-called burdens into dancing lights.

This is what I teach. I will show you how to tune in to your inner sanctuary of strength and knowledge through sense awareness. You have the ability to tap into this wealth of *knowing* at any time, and having that *knowing* is invaluable.

The discovery process is simple and even entertaining. Self-discovery can and should be a pleasurable experience, and this concept is gravely lacking in our culture. It is key to many of the issues our world faces today. The answers to the perplexing questions of life will not come from your clergy and for sure not your government. The answers lie within.

I say "The answers lie within," knowing fully that that is *no* new revelation, but I say it with renewed vigor. I say it because I am eager to show you just how true these words are. Exploring the intricacies of my inner world has been a passion of mine for years. It all began with learning a wonderful way to meditate. With this intriguing method of introspection, spending time in meditation took on an entirely new dimension. I learned while in silence. It became a hobby and a calling all rolled into one. What occurred was amazing. I was led to a new way of experiencing myself. I began seeing and feeling *me* from the inside out. My inner world became an inner stage—not visions created by thoughts, but visions created by sensations. There is a vast difference between the two. This love of observing the complete interior show is what I will share with you.

CHAPTER 6

HONORING THE PROCESS
OF LEARNING

For many years I meditated in the traditional manner, and like others, struggled with it but persevered. I used mantras and focused intently on the sound of the words and the meaning of the mantras. I followed my breath, altered my breath, held my breath, and although I did experience a variety of altered states, what I learned the most was how much I loved air! I sat with Buddhist monks in Thailand and *om*-ed with the best of them, and, of course, never lost sight of the objective: obtaining a clear mind, free of thought. I was thrilled and thankful when I finally came upon an infinitely easier and more effective way to go inward.

The evening that this new approach to meditation presented itself to me is still vivid in my mind. A group of friends and I were deep in meditation, having been soothed by the leader's voice as she channeled words that sounded like improvised poetry. Then she paused for a moment, which she had never done before, and encouraged us to be spontaneous and add to the moment if we felt so inclined. I am not even sure I had thought about it before, but out of my mouth came tones. Strong, deep tones that didn't sound like they belonged to me—no particular melody, no particular rhythm—the tones just flowed. I was unaware that others had joined me. It felt rather tribal and otherworldly at the same time. I was alive with vibrations and had the sensation that the energy I was feeling was visible. I felt that I was glowing. As the meditation ended, I was still spellbound and enveloped in a sphere of calming energy. Hardly anyone spoke as we filed out the door, and I could see in the others' eyes that they were moved as well. Everything pertaining to meditation and my life had changed that evening. It all sounds so simple—and it was.

I went to bed that night with feelings of excitement and anticipation swirling around inside me. I could not wait for the next day. Was it a onetime wonder or could I replicate it?

That next morning I went to my meditation chair with an eagerness I had never experienced before. I took one deep breath and let out a sigh. The noisy sigh felt awkward, but I kept it up until I finally made a good rich tone. I paused for a minute to see if anything had happened and I could sense the beginnings of the feeling from the night before. With no mantra or any other ritual confines, I was free to feel. The most extraordinary thing was the clarity of my mind—perfectly clear, in fact. With a few more healthy and whole-hearted tones, I was once again aware of my body and the energy stirring within me. I was so focused on feeling the vibrations I had unleashed inside me that I realized I could no longer feel my corporal body. All I could feel were an intense sense of peace and a vibrant light emanating from me.

I experimented with this new idea, and as I moved forward the inner doorways began to open. My daily routine was to tone for a bit, then stop and focus solely on how my body responded. Then I altered the sounds and observed the different feelings they produced. This was the beginning of many things, but mainly a brand-new relationship with me. I learned to be keenly attuned to my own vibrations and how all my senses related to them. I learned how I felt. Really felt. This came from my own vibrations—not something created by external vibrations from music, bowls, or drums. And I spent hours doing this because I loved it.

Over time I increased my awareness and heightened my senses to a new level, and the benefits were unbelievable. I began to feel the smallest of things in my body and learn from them. I learned that if I observed those sensations ardently and with a playful mind, I could go one step further and visualize them. For instance, what may have begun as a heavy and dark feeling in my body could become a bowling ball—a black bowling ball. When I stopped to tone, I noticed the energy level in my body rising. Once again returning to the visual, to my amazement, the bowling ball began to spin. As I stayed with the toning, the energy continued to build, and with each revolution the ball reduced in size until it disappeared. Not only was I aware of the wonderful benefit of no longer feeling the heaviness, but I also gained the understanding that I had power to alter my reality.

I found this new method of visual meditation to not only be a powerful tool for living a fuller life, but also an avenue for exploring and learning about the art of being human.

CHAPTER 7

ASKING YOURSELF THE HARD QUESTIONS

Is This a Bit "Woo-Woo" for You?

Before I move forward into the "how-tos" of this unfamiliar concept, let's address some of the naysayer thoughts that some of you might have roaming in your head.

When I say that we are going on an inner journey or when I speak of my inner world, you might find the words sound a bit too "woo-woo" or weird for you. I can assure you that it is only going to get worse! I say that to be funny, but it is also the truth. Remember it's just us and I won't tell anyone. What I will do is make your inner world blossom from a fertile ground of information, and as an added bonus, interesting to boot!

How Do You Get Along with Your World?

"How do you get along with your world?" may seem like an unusual question, but there are those who may not realize they live a life constantly at odds with their outer world. Being able to discern the difference between your outer and inner worlds is necessary to create the foundation for learning and understanding the real you versus the conjured version. If we are not able to sense the difference between our outer and inner worlds, we cannot differentiate between our true reality and the illusionary reality that we mistakenly feel is imposed upon us.

When You Shield Yourself from Pain, You Also Shield Yourself from Joy

At one time or another we can find ourselves feeling at odds with those around us or unhappy with life in general. A little bout of this doesn't hurt anyone, but many people take it to extremes. They have themselves convinced that their "outer world" is the enemy. They feel their happiness lies in the cards they are dealt and are quite sure the dealer is cheating. It follows suit (pun!), then, that they also find life as they see it as responsible for their ups and downs, and point their finger at it for what they call "bad luck."

This mind-set is common and can perpetuate itself. When we hear others grumble about the world around them, it feels normal to chime in with our complaints. My focus here is not on the discourse between people and their likes and dislikes, but on the habit of complaining and the effects it can have on the individual, his friends, family, coworkers, and ultimately all of humankind.

To have an outlook or opinion on life is our human nature, but where it becomes unproductive and harmful is when this skews daily interactions in a negative way.

When someone falls into this unseen trap, there is a deduction they typically make—they think, "It's not me that is the problem. If they had listened to me, all would have turned out perfectly." Wrong! That is not the way it works. A person who has a habit of nitpicking will find something wrong with the very best of conditions. They do this without thinking. They are unaware of how it makes them feel and affects those around them. They do it because it is a habit and they don't know how to break it. They are so attached to nitpicking they are not sure who they would be without it.

Let's take a look at this from another perspective. If someone told her that he knew where to find the source of her problems, and that in finding the source her life could become happier and more productive, would she be interested?

Do you think she would want to know where this place might be? Of course she would, but she would also be very skeptical and nervous about showing any interest for fear of what might be unearthed in her and what consequences could follow.

You can see that I have my job cut out for me. No matter how skeptical or apprehensive you might be, I can show you this is painless and easy and you are safe with me.

What Prompts You to Act and React

Here is an example of what I mean by outside and inside of you. It is so easy to overlook or disregard these intricacies. To shed more light on what I am saying, I will relate it to something we know and have in common. If you would please, take a look at these words: *action* and *reaction.* Now follow this logic: A person can take *action* without having any outside influence. So *action* originates from within. On the other hand, *reaction* requires a stimulus from the outside, and it is easy to claim that the stimulus caused you to react. But not so fast! The outside news, person, or thing may have come to your attention, but it did not evoke any kind of feeling or response. If you did choose to respond, your response came from how you interpreted what you just saw, felt, or heard. The things you react to are reflections of attitudes you have collected over time; or maybe it's heartburn. I know that sounds funny, but when we don't feel well we have different reactions to things than when we feel fit and in the flow.

The ability to take action or have a response to the outside world is healthy and necessary. Red light, foot goes to the brake. Telephone rings, you answer and say "Hello." Neither of these outside common occurrences should elicit a rise in blood pressure unless there is something going on inside you that causes an attitude to pop out. These everyday happenings go unnoticed. If, however, you are in a hurry or don't wish to be disturbed these interruptions or delays might create a wave of annoyance. If your emotions aren't too out of proportion to the cause and don't linger in the body too long, all is well. Our attention only needs to be alerted when the reaction is out of balance with the occasion, or the reaction attaches itself to an active attitude and hangs around for hours, days, or even longer. These offenders, or "attitudes with history," are chock-full of emotions. Each one of those little culprits is shaping your day, which is shaping your life.

If you are interested in knowing more about how you come to these actions and reactions, you must look within. So here we are again. If you want to change this behavior, you need to venture inward and take a look around.

You might ask, "How in the world could you ever make a change in a behavior that is so ingrained?" To be able to sort through what is initiating that which seems to be an automatic response is not an easy task. But it is one of many things you can see more clearly from the inside looking out.

Going inside is not difficult; it is acting on the choice to do so that can be hard. Just making that simple decision—taking time out and doing something really good for yourself—can be a big stumbling block for many people. I have seen it many times, so I know it warrants my bringing it up. You must decide to put yourself and your personal growth first. That means your list of things to do tomorrow starts with you and a chair.

Whether you find the thought of spending quiet time with yourself peculiar, too challenging, or everything else seems to be more important, keep this one significant thing in mind: if you want change in your life of any kind, or long to feel fulfillment, it must come from within.

How Do You Feel about Introspection?

Who looks outside, dreams. Who looks inside, awakens.

—Carl Jung

One time I opened a meditation session by saying, "We are going to begin our meditation by turning our attention to the sensations we have in our heads." One student remarked, "Oh, that sounds easy. I was afraid you were going to ask us to do something really hard, like try not to think or something." I can assure you that you won't have to worry about trying not to think. Your thinking side will soon become preoccupied with all the activity occurring on the inner level. The sensations of the body really are that captivating.

Our objective is to awaken your senses so you can feel again, like you did as a child. Your senses open a portal that you can enter. A step into that different space gives you an alternative way of viewing things. And with this new perception comes change.

To initiate change in your life, you start with spending more quality time with that person in the mirror. This takes me back to a line that I used earlier: "Your spiritual journey is as fruitful as you find yourself interesting." Since it is always easier to spend time with someone who is interesting, a good listener, and has a good sense of humor, my goal is to help you develop this kind of rapport with yourself.

If you haven't spent much time in introspection, there could be a raft of reasons why not. It could be that you're really not sure how to go about it, or you might think the exercise of inner-work would be too tedious and boring. Of course, there is always the possibility that you think you are perfect the way you are, and are just curious about what others are doing. Any perception of who you are or what you need is as important as another. There is no need for judgment or scrutiny of any position taken. You are the only one who knows, and it will be your sandbox, on your time. All it takes is a willingness to try. It will not be boring; it will be stress-free and very easy.

Do You Know How You Feel?

As we go inward, there will be no need to delve into your past. You will not ever encounter the word *why.* We are not looking for the whys of anything in your past, present, or future. But I will be using the word *how* quite often. What's the difference between using "how" instead of "why?" The answer is: Asking "why" makes you think; asking "how" makes you feel. I am taking a little liberty here in generalizing this statement, but I will clarify it more as we go.

Asking someone to describe how something feels engages her or him in a different way than when asking a question that starts with the word *why*. Therapists found this out ages ago, so they learned to use different phraseology to help elicit more of a response. But I have found a new reason about why "how" is so much more effective than "why," and this led me to create a methodology like no other.

Something very different happens when you ask people to convey their feelings without using words to describe their emotions, such as angry, sad, depressed, and others. If you ask them to describe *how* they feel by using their senses, their whole world changes.

Questions such as:

How would you describe the sensation that the emotion is creating in your body?
How would it feel if you could touch it?
Does it have shape?
Does it have color?
Can you feel its movement?
If you could hear it, what would it sound like?

shift our attention to something that we can articulate versus becoming mired in an emotional discourse that takes us nowhere. If you seek change in a negative emotion, it is through the senses that change can and does occur.

The ability to think is unique to our species, but *thinking* is not the gateway to experiencing fulfillment. In order to be in touch with our lighthearted, joyful selves, we need to turn the thinking way down and let our free-flowing senses have the floor. That same truth applies to creating a pathway to change. Stop and think about this for a minute. All I ask you to do is feel…allow the sensations that are already present in your body to become your center stage. This is a simple request, and when you do so you will find a treasure chest full of truths with your name on it.

Have You Given Your Thoughts Much Thought?

The thoughts that grip your mind also grip your heart.

It is common to have the belief…let me say that even stronger…we are *entrenched* in the belief that our thoughts are not within our control.

You will see this is not true. Thoughts have no substance and will disappear unless fed by your attention. That is why we want to keep our memory as healthy as possible so we can store things in our memory banks without having to recite them over and over again to remember.

It takes extra energy to keep repetitive thoughts alive. We have all done this, and it can be so annoying. Replaying a thought in your head commandeers useful energy needed elsewhere in your body. These types of thoughts are often negative, or scorekeeping, thoughts. If the repetitive thought were more useful, you would simply store it away in memory to be recalled when necessary. But the thought that you insist on repeating like a mantra with no end leaves you a victim of thought robbery. The thought keeps you at gunpoint and continues to wreak its havoc in your life, all the while usurping your body's energy. When you learn to be more aware of the sensations in your body, you can feel the tightness and tension it takes to keep a thought energized. For you to let go of the thought you must first feel its grip. Don't think it...*feel* it.

Learning to feel the smallest nuances of your body is where we are headed. What you will find is that your body is your teacher. You just need to learn to listen, feel, see, and hear it. That is what we are going to do...become reacquainted with your animal instincts. You will become aware of all the sensations in your body, and you'll do this in conjunction with meditation—seeing and feeling your way along your path.

Everyone seeks change in her or his life from time to time, whether a change in attitude or a change in a partner. What must happen to allow change in your life is for you to find the barrier that is keeping change from happening.

Talking about change is fruitless. Trying to figure things out is even worse. What does work is going inward to feel the sensations that the havoc has created. By giving your full attention to the sensations, you pull the plug on the energy used to feed the negative thought, which is fixated on the past or the future, and reroute it to the present moment. The act of being fully conscious in the present is what sets you free from that havoc and allows the change you seek. When that moment comes, there is a physical loosening you can actually feel. When the energy that has previously been stagnant begins to flow, you can feel it. Change lies in that stream of energy. Change lies in your ability to feel exactly where you are in the present moment, and to do that you must feel your body.

CHAPTER 8

CLARIFYING THE MEANING OF THE WORDS I USE

The meaning of many of the key words used in spiritual-ity books can be very subjective. Sometimes you can read an entire book and not really be clear what the author means when she or he uses certain words. I avoid that problem by giving you a list of the words and phrases I use and my personal definition for them.

The Ego

The first word on the list is *ego*, which I have purposefully not used until now. I did this so I could introduce you to the idea of watching your thoughts and feeling your body without other concepts to distract you. But I must include it here because you will see it many times from this point forward. And I make it my first word, because we cannot go further until we address it. I mean that more literally than you might think. The ego in you is the one that is already judging this book…and the ego needs to be satisfied that these words have value.

It is important to acknowledge that the ego, like all things in nature, has a positive and negative side or quality. The positive ego alerts you to your surroundings and is helpful as you navigate through your day. We are accustomed to the voice of the positive ego. It is the voice that speaks to us concerning daily matters like "You need your car keys," or "Turn off the stove," and although we are grateful for its promptings, its job virtually goes unnoticed. The negative ego is another story; it merits enough discussion for me to write this book. To simplify things, when I use the word *ego*, I am referring to the negative ego.

Defining what I mean by "ego" is vital to grasping the significance of my ideas, but I am not going to give you a one- or two-line definition for it. It is so unique and varied in its make-up that I will describe what it is and how it works throughout the pages to follow. I hold back nothing in telling you all I know and feel about this undisclosed yet pervasive character in our lives. It is a tad challenging to let the world see inside my head, but that is what it takes for you to see that what goes on in your head is not that different from the rest of humanity.

My goal is to tell you what I think the ego is, what it does, how it does it, and even why it behaves as it does.

As I said, I explore my understanding of the ego throughout the book, but as important as this word is we will move on to the other words in my lexicon.

The Difference between *Feel* and *Feelings*

To avert any confusion, let's get it clear: I will use the words *feel* and *feeling* many times.

"Feel" has two different meanings. It can mean an emotion or a sensation that you experience in your body. The word *feeling* pertains to physical sensations. If I speak of a feeling in the context of an emotion, I use the word *emotion.*

It is easy to confuse the act of thinking with feeling as well. So let's sort that out.

When you are thinking, you are often going over something that has happened in the past or rehearsing the possibilities of something that may or may not occur in the future. You are not always in the past or the future; there are those wonderful moments when you are in the present and you dialogue with yourself about what you are currently creating or seeing. Thoughts are simply words that are aligned to convey meaning, and are harmless in themselves. But when one of those words or scenarios connects with some logged piece of information, the response to that tidbit elicits an emotion.

The emotion could be one of thousands: joy, excitement, anger, sadness, or jealousy. We know these emotions by words. I want to go beyond the flat dimension of words and tap into the sensations that the words stimulate. Your body can feel things without the aid of thought, but much of what it feels is at the whim of your rambling mind. Emotions can attach themselves onto the thought or group of words, story, tale, or narrative, and be hard to shake.

Follow this logic:

If we think a thought and this triggers a past event that plays out in our heads, the memory, whether pleasant or unpleasant, spawns an emotion that causes the body to manifest a sensation.

So that is what you *feel*.

If our focus is locked on a thought that causes an emotion, we continue to have that feeling in our bodies. I'm going to be redundant here: When a chain of events takes place—when our focus gets locked on a thought that we continually repeat—that thought spawns an emotion, which creates a sensation in the body. The connection between the thought and the feeling or sensation in the body often goes unnoticed. You might observe this happening when you catch yourself repeatedly replaying a sentence or scenario. Most of the time this is steeped in negativity and the body reacts accordingly.

Funny but true, we ignore the body but we may become aware of the repetitive words. This is when your body needs your help because it cannot step out of that loop on its own. It is easy to fall into the belief that your thoughts have a life of their own and you have no control over them, and therefore no option. If you can stop for one second and realize that it is the thought, and the thought alone, that generates the negative feeling in your body, you have found your option. Once you identify the thought as the source of the crazy making in your body, you can choose to alter your course.

Having an option or choice changes everything. Just the thought that there might be another way frees up some energy. It is a good idea to use this new, free energy in a healthy and useful manner. Going inward is the most useful thing you can ever do when there is a choice to be made. Getting a clear picture from the inside out is key to the learning process.

Following the chain of events of thought-to-emotion-to-feeling-to-energy in slow motion and seeing it from an observer's point of view is our goal. We will simply look and feel our way into some amazing discoveries. As we move along, you will see yourself in the mirror of the pages. If I can with my words spur you to try what I talk about, the results will speak for themselves. Something I have discovered about us human beings is that our resistance to change is mighty and our willingness *not* to want to do something good for ourselves is even stronger. This, too, can change.

Vibrations

There is no need to rank these words according to importance, but if I did, this one would score extraordinarily high.

The meaning of "vibration" is rather commonplace, but it is not routinely used when talking about the body. The correlation between vibration and body has been lost because our ability to feel things in our bodies has been dulled. Our attention has turned to other things that are not so refined. But I am going to swing that pendulum back the other way as I focus our attention on the body and its senses.

As you know, feeling/touch is one of our senses. When we say we feel something, what we really mean is "I feel a vibration." When you touch a table, you know you have made contact with it because you feel something in your fingertips. That feeling in your fingertips is an exchange of energy in your body. The energy itself, on the smallest level, is vibration. In fact, everything that we experience as we interact with all existence is done so through the exchange of energy vibration. The reason you physically feel it is that the created energy oscillates as it travels. The oscillation causes vibrations. The sensation you feel when touching something is the vibration of energy in motion. All energy has movement and is in motion at all times. *Every part of you is in motion at all times.* One vibrational field is continuously interacting with another throughout your body. Many of the sensations are extremely subtle, so much so that we have become oblivious to them. We have dumbed down our sensory perception with TV, computers, and the other electronic devices. We have lost the ability to listen and learn from the wisdom that flows through our bodies on the very vibrations that we ignore.

We will recapture that lost art of being attuned to our bodies. We will turn our attention to the sensations in our bodies and feel the energy that life itself creates, which is vibrations. Feeling the sensations in your body is your gateway to learning. Feeling the vibrations, and knowing that you can create them, helps you comprehend how it is that you are the creator of your world.

Got it? You will.

Being in the Present

Being present is one of the single most important things we need to learn in order to master this life on Earth.

I have said to people in all seriousness that I really admire and feel for Jesus and how hard it must have been to get people to believe in something as simple as "The kingdom of Heaven is within." So sweet, so simple, and so true, but not an easy sell. For his teachings to penetrate the people around him, he had to embody those very words. His actions had to be congruent with his teachings. The living field around him had to be in tune with the words he spoke. This is also true of Buddha, Muhammad, Gandhi, and all the great spiritual leaders past and present.

Teaching truths is one thing, but living them in the day-to-day world is another. What these leaders acquired through their own observations on Earth was that the only perfection is in the moment. They themselves didn't require perfection, but learned to *see* perfection in allowing life to unfold. It was in their ability to be fully in the present moment that made them so captivating. Perfection only exists in the acceptance of the present moment...just as it is.

"Being present in the *now*" is the new, New Age buzz phrase, but as overused as it may be, the importance of it cannot be overstated.

If there is any drawback in the concept, it is that very few people really understand what "being in the now" means, and many who do would not be able to tell you how to go about knowing if they are in the now or not. There are many things this book offers, and one of the things I can guarantee is that when you finish reading and have tried the simple self-exploratory things I have come to love, you will *know* what "being in the now" is, and when you are there and when you are not.

Get ready to know yourself in a different way. You will find another dimension of life—one that has always existed within you, one that you may have happened upon but never given much credence. You will find the heart of you, the core of you, your Soul, and your eternal intent.

Toning

Toning is how people can add their vibrations to those of the universe without the constraint of words. It is free-form and natural. It is your unique sound, your audible thumbprint. Allowing that pure sound to come forth can be challenging in the beginning to some. Why? Simply because we have been asked to hold down the noise, especially those sounds that are unrefined or off- key.

Toning has been around since the beginning of time. It is a simple, handy, and personal tool that can be used to open the portal of transformation. Its history lies in ancient tribal chants, Gregorian chants, Tibetan chants, and Sanskrit mantras, just to name a few. All of these practices use the vocal chords to resonate tones, sometimes using words and sometimes not. But the purpose for each is the same: vibrations are created and one becomes immersed in the glorious sensations. If you hold your attention on that sensation, a portal opens, and you are welcome to pass through it and enter what I call the SilentPlace (see next definition).

To derive the most benefit from toning, there is a natural progression that must take place. First, you sigh. This loosens your vocal chords. Then you allow the sounds from within you to emerge. Once your tone has been given voice, you progress to the next step. At this point, you shift your awareness from *hearing* the sound to *feeling* it. To me this is "toning."

SilentPlace

I use the term *SilentPlace* when I speak of the place of balance and peace within. Although I talk about this space being inside you, it really has no boundaries. There is a doorway in, but once inside there are no walls. The conscious decision to surrender the material attachments of the ego takes you to the doorway, and once you have opened the portal and stepped inward, the entire dimension of reality shifts.

In the SilentPlace the earthly concept of duality disappears and is replaced with the simple experience of wholeness. It seems contradictory to say that you must you go within to find the SilentPlace when there really isn't a place that you go!

There is no specific location, but the sensation feels like you have moved inside your body to a peaceful place. And once inside, you are surrounded by the incredible soothing presence of the SilentPlace. It is everywhere. Your proximity to the warmth of grace can be felt throughout your whole body. In this place of equanimity, you encounter the archives of boundless wisdom. Your ability to perceive life from a different perspective allows your awareness process to be accelerated beyond your concept of time. That is what you will find in the SilentPlace.

Sixth Sense

When people speak of the sixth sense, they are usually referring to a paranormal or supernatural occurrence. The truth is we simply are not accustomed to being in tune with the meaning of normal or natural. We perceive that it is natural and normal for dolphins to sense earthquakes before they happen, or for tiny birds to navigate hundreds and hundreds of miles to the same destination every year, but our ego challenges us in our thinking that we are their equals.

Concepts such as those found in this book help the ego awaken to the realization that we, too, have the ability to know more than our thinking mind generates. We learn that we must enhance our intuitive skills through our senses. When we pass beyond relying solely upon our thinking as our superior guidance system and begin employing our natural sensatory capabilities, we will embark on unleashing the true potential of mankind. Each time we focus intently on tasting, hearing, smelling, seeing, or feeling, our connection to the matrix of the universe is completed. In that moment, we open the gateway to our Higher Power and wisdom—our sixth sense. And when we learn to use and trust this inner knowing, it becomes stronger and flourishes. Your sixth sense is innately yours and waiting on you to call upon it.

That completes the glossary of words. I found in the process of writing the comprehensive definitions that each one stimulates me with passion and respect for what is yet to come.

CHAPTER 9

UNDERSTANDING YOUR EGO IS ESSENTIAL TO KNOWING YOURSELF FULLY

Earlier I gave you my short definition of "ego." Now I will give you the broader, more fluid version.

I use *ego* to mean our lifelong companion, which parades in and out of our heads seemingly at will. It is the voice in our heads that demands attention, and its persistence is remarkable. Although we have more than one voice in our heads, the ego's voice stands out from the rest by its tone and attitude. I call it "the great mathematician," for it is always trying to add to, subtract from, multiply, or divide our lives into what it feels is more acceptable. But never, ever, is it satisfied with what is.

There is a part of the ego that is helpful. The positive ego alerts you to your earthly human needs such as letting you know that it is time to eat, that you need to go to bed, or that it's best not to have that next drink. But the helpful ego tips are delivered in quiet, subliminal messages and mostly go unnoticed; they are not seen as irritating or intrusive.

The part of the ego we will delve into is the polar opposite of the helpful ego. As a matter of fact, it can be downright overbearing, rude, and even shockingly hateful. It can say things that you are grateful no one else overheard, and you would dare not repeat.

The ego can be in command of our behavior and our lives if we do not take the time to get to know it and understand its objectives.

We will look at this intriguingly clever culprit, but we are not going to put it under the microscope and dissect it; we are going to befriend it. We are going to gain its trust.

Before we move on, there is another important element of our being that plays a part in how we approach life. It is the personality. It is easy for us to misuse the word *personality* when the word *ego* applies. The ego and the personality are two distinctly different facets of our makeup. They can easily become tightly entangled and very difficult to separate.

So how are they different?

Personality is the style or manner in which you approach life. You are born with it. The qualities of your personality can be inherited, but not always. Sometimes these unique qualities might be different from anyone else in your gene pool. A couple of examples of personality types would be an introverted or extroverted analytical or an introverted or extroverted intuitive. But in and of themselves, these types have no harmful or negative aspects. It takes the ego's tendency in assuming the role of protector, along with its infinite stash of unfavorable painful memories, to exert its influence on the different personality types. It can snare the clear thoughts of an analytical thinker and place the veil of fear over her or his eyes so they see all of life through the filter of anxiety. The ego can envelop an extroverted person with the veil of insecurities and cause her or him to move from being delightfully outgoing to dreadfully overbearing.

Our personality types are ours to have and to hold, but our ego is always changing. It is both our Achilles' heel and our whetstone. We need the ego's adversarial ways to aid in our advancement in understanding the human condition. We need it for contrast. We need it as a sparring partner to sharpen our spiritual skills. But to utilize the ego for our benefit, we must understand clearly the role it plays in our life. That is the direction we are headed.

The more I burrowed down to the core of my spiritual self, the more I became aware of how prevalent the ego was in the smallest details of my life. As a matter of fact, at times I felt I was comprised of nothing but ego. It seemed like my entire substance, the whole enchilada, was filled with nothing but the ego's wants, desires, and criticism. And at that time having nothing but enchiladas for the rest of my life didn't sound so *bueno*, and I love enchiladas. *No*, I was not capitalizing it then. It wasn't until much later that I developed an appreciation for the role the ego plays in our growth process and saw that it is key to our spiritual evolution. It was then that I started using the big "E" for Ego, so from here on it will be capitalized.

I won't ever capture in a simple sentence the meaning of something as pervasive and illusive as the Ego. Explaining what I feel it is requires examples and sharing of firsthand observations.

The meaning of the word *Ego* is expanding daily for me. It grows and evolves as my awareness broadens. The desire for coherence of the body, mind, and Soul is still the ultimate goal, but I have added a word to that neat little threesome and made it a foursome.

Mind*Ego*Body*Soul is a more accurate depiction of what is needed for humans to be in balance and harmony. The word *mind* is far too lacking in depth to encompass the entirety of what is needed to quiet the Ego's thoughts. To feel the balance that you seek in your daily life, you must include the card of the Ego to have a full deck.

This is not a trick; it really can happen. With Inner Vision Meditation we start with the Ego. We feel how the Ego manifests itself in our bodies. The tension that the Ego creates in the body provides a focal point. Becoming aware of that sensation is the first step in moving your attention inward.

When your attention is absorbed with feeling and you have allowed your sensation to be center stage, the mind becomes quiet. It is then that you can see, feel, hear, and even taste the pathway to the Soul. Learning this technique is not only possible, but also immensely helpful in navigating through the perplexity of being human.

Getting to know my Ego and learning that it is *not* the sole representative of my being is the single most important thing I have accomplished in this lifetime. In the process of watching my thoughts I was drawn to distinguish which of them caused feelings of compression and heaviness and which seem to flow forward with no negative feelings attached. I was interested in discerning more about the origins of the thoughts and so became an avid student of observation.

The step of becoming the observer might seem like a monumental task, especially if you are in the midst of an emotional upheaval. But the reality is that only the benefits deserve the word *monumental*. The act of becoming the observer requires only the slightest shift in perception. All that is necessary is a little curiosity, a dash of adventure, and a sufficient amount of desire.

I had these ingredients and diligently worked at my newfound interest. In time a wondrous thing happened. I uncovered the closely held knowledge of the ancient mystery schools: The observer in me was the "I" of me. I *was* the observer. I was the one seeing. I was not my thoughts. This unforeseen awakening opened doorways for me that were previously obscured by lack of understanding. The doorways opened inward and once inside I found a vast new world beckoning me to continue my quest for knowledge.

I felt, I watched, I listened, and from the advantage point of the observer, I could see the interaction of the Ego and the self. I saw the origin of the thoughts that brought me pain and those that brought me joy. A treasure chest of life's precious secrets was there for me to discover, and the process of learning about the Ego held the key to that chest.

CHAPTER 10

HOW I CAME TO MY IDEAS

Because the Ego is so important, I will share with you how I came to see it as such a vital part of the spiritual equation. Retracing my steps is not something I am fond of doing because I am now very much of a "Now" person! But I wasn't always. The best way to substantiate the premise of my philosophy is to explain how it unfolded for me in real time.

Once upon a time… (I had to do that!) No, sincerely, I must go back to the beginning for this to make sense.

As a child I don't recall ever making a decision to follow the spiritual path; I was born into it. My mom played a huge part in every facet of my life, but especially esoterically. She was on the cutting edge of New Age thinking, and she was an endless source of inspiration and knowledge for me. To add a little spirit fuel to the mix, my formative years were during the era of "make love not war," inner explorations, and seekers of ancient wisdom. My family attended the Unity Church in Houston, when it was held at Theater, Inc., and Reverend Newsome was in the pulpit. He was my hero and the *Daily Word* was my guide.

In my early teens, my personal objective was to become grounded and at peace at all times, nonjudgmental of myself and others, and a presenter of loving-kindness to all humanity. Sounds like a lofty goal, but I thought if I became enlightened enough I would reach the place of Nirvana here on Earth. As a child this was a fun ambition, but as I got older it seemed further out of reach. Striving toward this ideal usually did nothing more than make me feel guilty for having failed.

What did I do? I learned more and tried harder. Going for various styles of massages (known then as bodywork), doing breath work, getting my astrology chart done or Tarot cards read was a once-a-week event.

Then there were the books; I loved them so. Books like *I'm OK, You're OK*; *Primal Scream*; *There Is a River*; *Jonathan Livingston Seagull*; *Seth Speaks*; and, of course, the classics from Kahil Gibran. They were great at inspiring me to keep trying to become more pure and less judgmental. But what was that niggling thing that was always present? What was that voice that made me feel unworthy or guilty for having negative thoughts?

Yes, you guessed it: the Ego.

Some of the books I read addressed the Ego, but still not in a clear, straightforward way. They left me with the idea that if I were to strive harder I could mollify or completely overcome the Ego, and that would happen when I became more grounded, more loving, and more kind. There was an idea du jour for ways to expel the Ego: I could paint it, shout at it, drown it in tears, make it a pillow and talk to it, or try smudging it out of my life. I did each of these things more than once, and although they really did leave me feeling changed and uplifted, the Ego was right back on duty in no time.

I then moved from "banish the Ego" to "give the Ego its voice." The idea was to own the Ego's negativity and express it. The negative Ego was also referred to as the Shadow or the Dark Side. Keeping the Ego hidden was thought to give it strength to do its dirty work. Owning it meant to admit to or uncover the negativity that lived beneath the surface of an otherwise smiling face.

I was told that I smiled a lot, so I thought that meant I must have bucket loads of this negativity lurking down below. The plan of excavation sounded good to me, so I went to work unearthing all the negative culprits I could find inside. Then I conducted a self-confessional and proclaimed my deep, dark secrets into the mirror. Thing is, they weren't too terribly juicy, and I didn't feel much catharsis having shown them the light. Of course, I assumed that I had not burrowed deeply enough and that there was still a hidden monster left inside.

What I *did* like about this approach was that I felt I was less in opposition to the negativity or the Ego that I did encounter. That was a much better than seeing it as the number one enemy and trying to extinguish it. It was beginning to become clear to me that the Ego—or at least mine—was going to be around for the long haul.

But I still felt there was something lacking in my understanding of my Ego. I owned all the darkness I could find and yet I did not feel any shift in my life. More often than not, this lack of change left me feeling like a failure at my spiritual practice, and I *knew* that couldn't be right. It had to be possible for me to feel peace and joy without the Ego usurping my energy.

I continued on my path but not with any design in mind. I was just following my nose, so to speak. I had no idea where the next turn was taking me…I just knew I was going. I was aware that something out there was going to open the spiritual doors for me, and I was ready—really ready.

It was in 1980 that I made the decision to temporarily leave my true love and my job and enrolled in Lomi training in Marin County, California. Lomi is a type of bodywork like no other. This training was not the Lomi Lomi of today, but a cross between Gestalt therapy and Rolfing. The teachings were intense and encompassed many different areas to prepare me to be with people as they released emotions during the bodywork.

We started each day with a one-hour meditation. Yikes! One hour with me and my Ego? If the instructors had a specific meditation technique, they did not share it. As I look back, I see they wanted us to walk over the hot coals by ourselves and find our own way. This was the beginning of really getting to know my Ego; and at that time I was still desperately wishing I could give it the slip.

In six months of training, I never had a single moment of bliss during meditation. But I did learn that I had many different voices in my head, and I could tell which one (or ones) was the voice of the negative Ego. Its voice always had edginess and it wanted to do anything rather than sit still and be quiet. Sometimes I could track by its banter where the Ego was headed, and other times it seemed to conjure things out of thin air just to keep me on my toes. Even though I did not reach the joy of silence, I certainly got the hang of hanging out with my thoughts.

After the training ended, we had one more task to complete before we were certified. I had to return to the trenches and attend an eleven-day silent meditation. Help! I thought. What am I to do? I had endless hours once again of waiting for the bliss to hit…and then finally, finally! a change began to occur. I found that I was engaging myself in not only listening to the Ego's voice, but also observing its style and mannerisms. I noticed all of its mood swings. I could see which topics it liked to focus, or, rather, gnaw on the most. I watched it flounder from one thing to another in its quest to remain the center of my attention. I could feel how sensitive it was to being challenged. I could feel how the past was its nemesis and the future its phantom foe. I could see, sadly, how brutally mean it could be. From this perspective, I could just sit and let it be the show. As I became more involved in the observation, the amount of time required in that session became less of an issue and that was a tremendous relief, but something else was happening, too.

As I watched my thoughts, I began to notice that my body was reacting to the words I was hearing in my head. If I thought, "Oh, no, we have another twenty minutes more of sitting," a rush of heat would accompany those words. I could feel my face tighten and then my jaw began to clench. I would track the sensations starting with the origination point and then see how far it spread throughout my body. The intensity and variety of the body's reactions fascinated me. I became mesmerized by them and watched them like you would watch a mischievous new puppy.

I wasn't just thinking Ego thoughts anymore—I was seeing their effect on me.

I had listened to these voices all my life and thought they were *me*. Now I was seeing that not everything I heard in my head was representative of me or my true values. I could see that my Ego appeared to have an agenda of its own and feel the effect it was having on me.

The more I observed this phenomenon, the more astounded and baffled I became. Astounded at how much influence this nonsense chatter had on me and baffled at how something so pervasive and universally common to all humanity was not talked about. Not only is it not talked about, it is literally swept under the carpet.

Just think about it. It is common knowledge that everyone has DNA more alike than it is dissimilar. Every small detail of our biological system is studied and discussed at length in the medical world. There are research projects that track the processes of the mind and follow our thoughts from impulse into action. But here is an enigmatic fact: We have this unceasing Ego thing going on in our heads and it is very rarely discussed. You would think that the endless, pointless prattle that persists in our heads would get a mention or two. Not only is this universal inner annoyance never a topic of conversation, but at times we would rather be forced to watch reruns of *Liberace* than admit to the thoughts that just passed through our minds. Most of us don't know the origin of the voices and have come to accept them as some kind of personal affliction that we must endure.

In short, we have allowed an entity that we know very little about to play a huge role in our lives. We have become abjectly accustomed to it, but certainly not immune.

I found this perplexing issue with the Ego fascinating. So much so, that I decided it was time to bring my Ego out of the closet and take a closer look at it. This turned out to be a very liberating experience. Any time I noticed the Ego chiming in with its critical review of my actions, I acknowledged it. I would actually say, "Hello, Ego." This small act of awareness blossomed into a tool that helped me not only to see the Ego when it popped out its head but also gave me a way to objectively observe it. I began to be able to see it, recognize it, and understand it more clearly. This was exciting, but I was still left with important questions: How did the Ego get so strong? Why does it take such a cynical view of life? and Why is it there in the first place?

I did not know it at the time, but I was about to learn the answers to these questions and more.

I learned the Ego was much, much more than just the domineering, self-centered old biddy I heard in my head. I discovered that the Ego serves a valuable purpose and has performed an indispensable role in the development of humankind. All I needed to do was to open my eyes and ears and absorb what was in front of and inside me.

In order to acquire more knowledge about the Ego, I needed to give it my full attention rather than trying to function in spite of it. I had attempted to walk through my life while ignoring the ball and chain that seemed to be attached to my brain—and there had to be a better way.

Through meditation I observed the Ego, rather than be in its grip. The Ego can be intriguing when you witness its antics from an objective lookout point, but the real advantage is being able to feel its attack and then feel what it leaves in its wake. This objectivity initiated a new relationship between me and the stranger within.

This process of differentiating which emotions are initiated by the Ego and which are natural and healthy responses are not only paramount to leading a self-fulfilled existence, but an essential component of our growth. This awakening is necessary for our species to move forward. Learning to identify the role of the Ego in our lives and then expanding that awareness to how it affects our culture is the ultimate goal. Bringing this part of our existence to light is vital to humankind's evolution; but have you ever considered that our evolution is essential to the evolution of the universe? Yes, humanity is an important cog in the Big Wheel.

Humankind's Collective Ego

Because most of us have yet to discover the Ego and understand the reason behind its ways, we as a society still listen to its voice and fall under its self-appointed rule. The Ego has learned that it rules best by inflicting shame, guilt, and fear. If you think about your Ego and how it can torment you at times, and then magnify that by the number of people on Earth, you can see the basis of the turmoil we have in the world today. And yet I say this: The Ego does not have to be given the throne or the power to be the ruthless dictator of our lives or our world. Books like this one and other methods of awareness will awaken people, and where there once were shadows looming in the dark…there will be light.

This is how life unfolds—it is a process that we must honor, rather than endure.

Some find it easy to lay blame on humankind for all life's problems. They go so far as to say humans are inherently evil. This could not be further from the truth—no truer than that a child is evil for painting the bathroom with lipstick.

There are also those who would claim that all suffering has been caused by a massive glitch in the "master plan," which is a result of us—aberrant humans—falling from grace. This is another example of the Ego's contrivance and its great ability in dishing out shame and guilt.

I believe that everything on Earth and in the universe is evolving, and that includes human beings. Yes, we have free will, which places us in a unique category of our own, but that does not exclude us from the natural recycling and transforming process of all things. The numerous theories that profess something has gone *wrong* with an otherwise perfect plan just do not feel right to me.

To put it as succinctly as I can: My way of honoring that there is indeed a Higher Power is by *not only* claiming, but by knowing that no part of me is a mistake. Yes, humans create chaos, and, yes, we have a lot to learn and maybe a long way to go, but we are *going*. I know I am *going* and I am not alone.

CHAPTER 11

THE MYTH OF THE EGO

When I shifted my thinking from the Ego being my obstacle to understanding it and even befriending it, I could see past its masquerade of "do-gooder" and into its single-minded nature. I feel the Ego is here to do a job for us and almost *never* takes its eye off the ball. I say "almost never" because as we get further into Inner Vision Meditation, you will see that it can relax, even learn. But the day I learned that the Ego had a job to do and therefore a purpose, I felt liberated from a battle I was never to win.

When you look at the Ego as part of your *being* here on Earth and see that it has a designed purpose, your attitude toward it and your life begins to change. I believe this wholeheartedly, and that viewing life through the lens of this concept holds great promise for all of us. It can be a turning point for us as individuals as well as mankind as a whole.

To illustrate how I feel the Ego came into being and how it evolved into the position it holds in our lives today, I fashioned the following fairy tale–like story. It has a mythic resonance and yet I feel it is not far from being as it was and as it is.

The Ego and the Soul

When mankind first began evolving on the third planet from the sun, s/he was given an inner guardian. The guardian knew nothing of universal consciousness nor did it have the ability to conceive of the precious inner spirit that dwelled within its earthly body. What it did have was something enormously important and essential in the evolution of this sacred species. This caretaker and protector was adept at acclimating to the physical world. This was vital to humankind's ability to survive, thrive, and evolve.

This guardian was called the Ego. Its sole job was to nurture and protect the physical body of this being. The Soul Spirit that resided within waited patiently for the evolution of its earthly companion. There was a timing issue of readiness that the Soul knew to honor.

In the beginning, the Ego was a blank slate. It had no predecessor, no history, and no manual. What the Ego did have was an excellent processor called "the mind." It learned quickly from trial and error. It learned from what it observed and experienced.

Manning and operating the lookout post for the body was an ominous job and made even harder by the constant dangers that prevailed. The first skill to be mastered was one of survival. From all that the Ego could see or comprehend, it was alone in its efforts to stay alive. It, and for good reason, quickly assumed that it was solely responsible for the life or death of its body and assumed the positions of the gatekeeper and king rolled into one.

As in any species, humans became more adept at staying alive as they evolved. It was then that the Soul's Spirit within began to stir. Like the Ego, the Soul also had a purpose and a plan, and a grand plan it was. The Soul was a wave of Divine Spirit that had been placed inside each being. This was the essential element needed for evolution to move forward…for God had taken a part of himself and placed it in the body of man for the sole purpose of creating the sacred bridge between matter and consciousness. In time, this all-important bond would unveil the mystical link between consciousness and creation. And with all things being in the flow of evolution and the All being God, this plan was of great importance.

The body of mankind provided an avenue for Spirit to experience itself—to hear its own echo. Mankind became God's reflection in the mirror. It was in that first glance that consciousness was infused into matter, and in doing so added the senses of the body to the vast arena of universal power.

The Soul in mankind evolved as part of the divine plan and was imbued with the ability to create as the Creator creates. The process was in place for the Ego to protect the vessel where it dwelled, and over time the Ego would learn to honor the Soul. The difficulty of this task was no mistake. This enormous mission would take diligence and patience, and had no restraints of time. No undertaking this important, this crucial, this vital to the evolution of all things could be expected to take less.

Since the Ego responded only to what it could see and touch, the sum of its learning process had been spent in the posture of defense. Fear was the Ego's constant companion, but the Ego's body was perfectly designed and learned quickly the art of survival. In time, humans had moments where they could rest and even had time to reflect on their existence. This was the opening the Soul needed to let its presence be known.

This moment was sacredly historic. It signified the awakening of consciousness in humanity. It was the moment in time when the sacred bridge began to develop—the bridge that was needed for the Soul to cross over and lead the fear-gripped Ego to the trust and truth of its origin.

In order for the Soul to fulfill its mission on Earth, it needed to work slowly and diligently with the Ego; it needed to utilize the skills of its God nature to win the confidence of the naysayer Ego. Because the Ego could not see or touch the Soul, the Soul would have to find ways to teach the Ego. The Ego would have to experience the Soul by feeling the Soul's inner strength and by listening to its soft voice. The Soul would need to display to the

Ego that it could provide a source of protection that was invisible and yet expansive, invincible, and unending.

Then the Soul would share its universal sacred wisdom with the earthly Ego and be the Ego's escort. With the Soul's intrinsic grace and rhythm it would unwearyingly await the precise moment of opportunity to guide the Ego to the higher levels of perception. From this elevated position, the Ego would be able to glean the understanding and awareness it had deeply longed to touch since its inception.

The master plan was for the bond between the Ego and the Soul to become strong and founded in trust. With the assistance of the life eternal Soul, the Ego would awaken to its original design and purpose. The Ego would continue its responsibilities as the body's director of earthly affairs, but no longer have to feel alone in its role of being the sole line of defense. The Ego would then no longer be a haven for darkness for it would no longer live in fear of life or death.

It is then that the sacred bridge will be complete and the evolution of all things will move onward to the next cycle of becoming the unknown.

The cornerstone of this belief is that the Ego is paramount to our spiritual growth and vital to our existence here on Earth. In a practical sense, the Ego is the maintenance engineer and the scout for our bodies. It provides all the useful information that our sacred self needs to survive in this three-dimensional world. Without the Ego we would not be able to function. The Ego is the gatekeeper of the body, but it is not static or fixed *and this is the most important part of all*: it can evolve.

The Ego is as much a part of universal evolution as is a tiny sparrow or vast galaxies. This allows us to include the human condition in the process of evolution, and that feels good, rather than holding onto the theory that something has gone wrong with God's plan.

In spite of its mystical fairy-tale ring and that it may seem too far out of man's reach, I have witnessed the Ego releasing its grip on the most unsavory shame and guilt, so why not believe it can do more and more…each day…each year…each life. This tale of the Ego might hold more truth than we know.

I know this part is true for sure…there is a journey to be taken and I am on it and I would like you to join me.

CHAPTER 12

AWAKENING YOUR SENSES

This whole process of exploration is based on your willingness to be real and completely honest with yourself. Being a good researcher of self requires the deft skills of being a good playmate. I mean this—yes, playing. We have been stuck in the role of acting and reacting for so long that we have developed habits that keep us confined to being who we are not.

In this new inquiry of self, you will be asked to break away from the old habits, to color outside the lines with a new and creative methodology. The Ego resists change and is very tenacious. That is why you must allow your authentic self to stretch outside its preconceived boundaries. Once you free yourself from the Ego-imposed restrictions, you will be able to open the closed gates of the Ego and behold the precious sight of your true self.

Maybe this sounds like hype to you, but you'll see that you can learn clever new ways to maneuver yourself through the Ego's maze—a maze created by those old, worn-out habits. You will learn to break those habits rather than be held hostage by them.

Allow your time spent with the self to be light of spirit and fun. No one else is looking or can feel your inner world but *you*. There is no one to judge you. This is your space—yours alone and what you find is yours to keep.

We begin our exploration of the senses by focusing our attention on hearing. It is an easy and simple thing to do, and yet a great deal can be learned in a very short length of time.

When I refer to our senses, hearing, of course, is one of them. But what I want to bring to your awareness is not your ability to hear, but your ability to *listen*. There is a clear distinction between the two.

You may think you listen just fine, but as you will see after this short lesson that your listening capacity can be altered greatly by intent and concentration.

We don't realize how much we have filtered and synthesized the sounds around us. We are accustomed to listening with Ego judgment thoughts jumping in and out of our heads and we are unaware that this process is happening. The sound or sounds become rearranged to the Ego's liking, and our receptivity to the true resonance of the vibrations is gone. We view ourselves as being only a recipient of the incoming vibrations and we eliminate ourselves as part of the experience.

In order to get the full effect of this lesson, sit outdoors. I want you to approach this moment as if you have recently been given the gift of hearing and you have saved this moment to go outside and experience the sounds of nature for the very first time.

Here we go…

Step One: Finding Your Place

Be aware of your needs and find a comfortable place, one where you can lean back and stay for a bit. The Ego will want you to go inside if it is too hot, too cold, too windy, too… So take care of all of your needs before you begin. Tell those who might need to talk to you or need your help—and that includes your animals—that you are going to be out of touch for fifteen minutes. You really want the freedom to be totally immersed in what you hear while being outside.

Step Two: Surrendering to Gravity

When you first sit, don't be concerned with listening. Just adjust yourself to your spot and surrender to the gentle pulling sensation of gravity. Piece by piece let gravity have its way with you until you feel there is no more resistance in your body.

Step Three: Adding Your Breath

Take a small breath and feel the air as it moves in through your nose and out your mouth when you exhale; feel the air as it moves across your lips. Repeat this several more times. There is no rush here and no exact way to breathe. The only importance is being in touch with what you are doing by feeling the sensations the air makes as it enters and exits your body.

Now take a deep breath, one that creates a gentle *shush*-ing noise in your nostrils. Hold it for a brief moment and then exhale out your mouth with pursed lips, and once again create the *shush*ing noise with the exhaled air.

Now take an even deeper breath, breathing in through your nose and exhaling out through your mouth, letting the air make an even louder *shush*ing noise as it leaves. Play with this by altering the shape of your mouth while at the same time paying attention to different sensations you feel as the air passes through your lips. You will notice that each shape not only makes a different sound, but also feels different.

The Ego may be passing judgment on you and confining the movement of your face. Be resolute about being child-like! Let your lips be pronounced in their movement.

Step Four: Listening

Next, turn your attention solely to listening to the sounds you are making. Listen to the rush of air as it moves inward and outward…in and out, in and out. Listening, listening, listening. Continue doing this until you feel you have truly locked on to the ability to listen to your breath.

Pause and breathe gently and just relax.

Now turn your attention from the sound of your breath to *all* that you hear in your surroundings. (As a side note, you might even feel a sense of movement as your mind transfers from inner focus to outer attention.)

Let your mind do what it does best: Let it pick out and identify the different sounds that you hear. At first it might seem like they all are coming from different locations.

There could be a variety of sounds, but the loudest one will attract your attention and the others will become background noise.

Ego Interference

When you think you have included all the sounds around you, notice if your Ego has placed judgment on any of them. If so, the Ego will make that sound louder and the others will fade away. The reason this occurs is that the Ego is interspersing thoughts while you are listening. The Ego thoughts generate the attitude about the sound.

The way to listen without the judgment of the Ego is to turn your attention solely to the vibration the sound creates. (If necessary, refer to my definition of vibrations on page 37.) This takes an attention muscle that you may not have exercised before. It will help if you allow the vibrations to seem tangible, as if you could actually see them traveling from their origin to your ears. It enhances the experience, so try it.

Judgment of sound diminishes when you focus on the vibrations of the sound and not the thought that tries to block it.

This is a powerful way to learn this simple basic truth:

It is a thought that creates the attitude that creates the day.

Step Five: Playing

This next step takes a bit more concentration. Let the softer sounds come to the forefront. Then play with shifting your attention back to the loudest sound, back to the softest sound, and back to the loudest sound. In doing so, you allow each one to be the star of the show.

Now permit all the sounds to be equal. See, feel, and hear them. Include your heartbeat into this symphony of sounds. Pretend that your heartbeat is the timpani drum keeping rhythm for the entire orchestra. This requires your imagination, and you cannot fail. Whatever you develop in your head is yours alone. Pretend the sounds are there just for you. Play with the sounds as if they were your toys.

Now comes the part I love the most: When you have spent some time listening and playing with what you hear, you will have ceased to think—that is, unless the Ego pops in with judgment again. See if you can observe when you are listening and when you are thinking. Let me state this in a more emphatic way: *When you are thinking, you are not listening.* This means that as soon as a thought crops up in your head, you have stopped listening. This is the first time you will experience the phenomenon that when you keep your intent on *feeling* the sounds, your thoughts step aside and allow you to hear, truly hear. That is the difference between hearing and listening!

What You Have Learned

Now that you have spent time in what you perceive as your command center (the *head*), you have learned that you can move the focal point of your attention from one spot to another. You can stretch your ear to hear a sound far in the distance and in the next second bring it all the way back to hear your heartbeat.

You did this by following the sound vibrations on the outside to the inner vibrations of your heartbeat. When you performed this task, you began by using your sense of hearing and then added your feeling sense. In so doing you heightened your awareness by fine-tuning your sensory perception. This sounds so simple, but in fact we rarely exercise our senses and as a result, our world has become smaller and less engaging. To exploit an overused phrase even further, we have become dumbed down and, therefore, immune to what is around us.

This exercise prepares you to move on to the next step in learning a powerful new way to be present in your world.

CHAPTER 13

THOUGHTS HAVE FEELINGS, TOO

We can describe how things feel that occur outside our bodies such as hot, cold, hard, heavy, and rough, but we are not accustomed to describing how things feel on the inside. You will find that your inner sensations don't differ much from outside sensations, but to describe them you must rely upon an inner imaginary sense of touch.

In this chapter we are going to activate that inner imaginary sense of touch so that your sensations become your living guide. We are also going to introduce the idea of Inner Vision Meditation. To accomplish this you need to use your tools of imagination and intuition.

Although the previous chapter on listening was soothing as well as insightful, we were merely knocking on the front door to the depth of the meditation to come.

Let's begin.

Step One: Finding Your Spot and Gathering Your Things

Once again locate your spot for sitting. (Keep in mind that when you learn this technique you will be able to meditate almost anywhere; for now, establish a meditation spot that you can return to daily.) The place that might work the best may surprise you. You might think that the spot you picked outside would be a good location and sometimes it is, but you want this place to be easily accessible and user-friendly. Sometimes an extra bedroom that you rarely use is good. Small places can feel cozy, so don't discount a large closet or utility room. Add a chair and you're set.

If you happen to have two crystals, put them near the chair. I love crystals and feel that holding one in each hand promotes balance and conducts energy. If you do not have crystals, find two small symbolic things and hold one in each hand. You can have fun shopping at a later date for just the right crystals.

If you are curious why I have you hold something in each hand even if they are not crystals, the reason is simple—it gives your Ego a sense of security and lets you go about your task.

A candle adds atmosphere but is not a necessity. You can be the judge of whether you have the time or inclination to light one.

When you decide the time is right and you have fed the dogs, let the cat in or out, put your cell phone out of earshot, and turned off the TV, make a list of the things that are on your mind that you think you might forget and put down the list.

Now you are ready to go sit, but on your way grab a Kleenex. You never know.

Step Two: Sitting Down

Place your feet flat on the floor. Many of us are accustomed to sitting with our legs crossed, but this is a form of holding on, so let your feet fall to the ground. Some of you have mastered sitting in the traditional meditation posture. I would say suit yourself, our objective here is to feel comfortable and bodily free. If that posture is easy for you and you can maintain the sensations throughout your body while sitting for a spell, then please, Buddha up.

However you choose to sit, it is important not to slouch. This is not because of some posture rule, but because if you allow yourself to slump in the chair you will lose some of your vibrations and sensations to the pillows or cushions. Be stingy with your sensations; you want to feel every one of them. I don't want you to feel stiff, I want you to be comfortable and alert to your body. If while sitting your feet do not touch the floor, put a pillow underneath them so that you feel grounded.

Place the crystals or symbolic objects you have chosen in each hand. Now that you are sitting, do nothing more in the way of preparation.

Step Three: Sorting Out Your Doubts

You may find yourself thinking, "I can't do this. I have too many thoughts in my head." You may feel excited, nervous, or even afraid. My response to that is, "Good!" The more thoughts and energy you have, the more you have to lead you inward. Let it all come. Whatever the flavor of your thoughts, let them flow because the next step is to center your attention on how the thoughts feel. I know this puts a new twist on things, but it is exactly what I mean.

Step Four: Using Your Inner Senses to Feel

Close your eyes and sense the activity that you feel in your head. Be open to letting all possibilities exist. You may not have been asked to do this before, so let me say you are looking for the tiniest of sensations. Do not disregard anything. Any and all things about you count and are to be included. You may have a sense of what you see on the backs of your eyelids or maybe a faint shadow effect that seems to move somewhere in the background of your head. Whatever is there feel it. Nothing is insignificant.

You will be aware of impulses. Each thought you have creates a flicker of energy and with each one comes an almost imperceptible feeling of activity. Ignore the content of the thoughts and simply feel what kind of motion, however minute, the thoughts create in your head when they are un-leashed from who knows where.

Feel the sensations that are created as the thoughts come and go. Feel their movement and see if you can detect any pulses of light or color. Play with them by using your imagination. Do not concern yourself with the subject matter of the thoughts, only how they feel and where they are located.

To show you how diverse your sensations may be, here are a few questions to stimulate your awareness. Knowing what something is not helps you know what it is.

Do the sensations seem to form a cluster at the top of your head?

Are they gathered in one side of your head or the other?

Do they dart about?

Do they swirl in circles?

Let it be a game of finding them and feeling them.

Do they seem to originate from deep within your body?

Or do they come from out of the blue?

Is the inside of your head splotched with color?

Or are there black-and-white wavy lines, like an EKG?

These examples give you an array of things to inspire you to see and feel your personal brain print for the day. If you say you feel nothing and see nothing, however, do not be put off. Observe the nothingness. Allow yourself to see the blank screen.

Is the blank screen the same shade of dark all the way across?

Watch for the smallest nuances. Be patient with yourself. See if you can detect the slightest movement on the screen. Be open to what you see or don't see. Be open to allowing exactly what is. Be sensitive to all sensations.

In this exercise, what is true for you in your present moment is all that is important. Your only task is to be the observer. Let the activity be the show no matter how bold or slight.

You will likely be enticed once again to wander into the act of thinking through the subject matter of your thoughts. You may even be drawn into the act of analyzing the situation, but *remember* that your job is only to be the observer of sensations, not of thoughts.

Continue being the observer for a few minutes and then stop.

Step Five: Learning to Shift Your Attention

In Step Four we concentrated on the sensations, which eliminate thinking. Now I want you to deliberately think. You might find that it is difficult to begin to think again. After tossing around a couple of thoughts, maybe even a juicy one or two, return to observing the sensations in your head. You may have created additional sensations, even brand-new ones, or you may have returned to a quieted mind with very little observable activity. Whatever is there for you, be with it for as long as you wish.

When you are ready, open your eyes.

When you make this transition from daydreaming or unattended thinking to observing the activity inside your head, you can actually feel the sensation of movement. More important is to see that you have control over where you place your focus. Along with learning that you are able to maneuver your attention from one thing to another, you may see that you can choose to *think* or choose to *feel*. *You have now seen proof that you are not your thoughts. Not only are you not your thoughts but you have a wonderful, knowing self inside, which can guide you through selecting those thoughts that are beneficial and those that are not.*

CHAPTER 14

MOVING DEEPER INTO INNER VISION MEDITATION

There is something very important and wonderfully different about Inner Vision Meditation. This technique teaches you to allow your bodily senses be your guide. By starting the meditation in the present moment and letting your sensations come to the forefront, you develop a new way of tuning in to your spiritual self. You learn a new way of learning.

I can explain it best this way: When I see my new clients trying to place themselves in a meditation posture and immediately begin deep breathing to prepare themselves for meditation, I ask them to hold up. I tell them they are going to miss the best part. It is extraordinarily important to begin meditation by acknowledging the body in its Now state, as we have just done.

If you move into meditation without acknowledging the body, you miss your body's clues and cues. If you ignore the body, you miss the point of living in a corporal form. The body is our teacher and will lead us inward in a way that is profoundly meaningful and enormously important.

I cannot emphasize this enough.

What we have learned from the previous chapter was how to sense the sensations in our head by using our inner touch and our Inner Vision.

Now we will expand upon those skills and move our attention to the entire body. Let the sensations in your body be guideposts—guideposts that assist you in discovering more and more about you.

Step One: Sensory Scan

It is time to return to your special meditation spot. Be attentive to your posture, place your crystals or special objects in your hands, and, without altering another thing, close your eyes.

As before, feel for sensations, and this time, scan your entire body for anything that draws your attention. Treat what you feel in that moment as being of the utmost importance.

Here is a list of sensations that are commonly described by other meditators:

- Heavy feeling in the chest
- Tightness around the head, neck, or shoulders
- Hot sensation in the throat
- Pervasive heaviness throughout the body
- Tightness in the jaw

Your sensations could be completely different from these examples, but whatever the sensations are, they are yours and worth keeping for observation.

Step Two: Focusing Your Attention

Next is more than just noticing what your sensations are—you will examine them. Pick the sensation that stands out from the others and focus on it. When you become aware that your mind has wandered away to other things, bring yourself back to the task at hand. Refocus your attention on the sensation.

There is a good chance the sensation may not be pleasant; and it may feel foreign to bring to the forefront a feeling you would normally want to ignore or make go away, but do not try to alleviate the discomfort. Appreciate the sensations in your body as you would a direction sign pointing toward your destination.

Take baby steps as you go about the process of allowing the feelings in your body to be revealed and acknowledged. Sometimes we become so distanced from our body that when we turn our attention to it and allow ourselves to feel, it can be overwhelming. It is possible the sensations are very intense and seem to say, "Don't come near me." If this is the case, stay with it and keep your focus.

If you find yourself judging whether you are doing the lesson correctly or judging the sensations themselves (as in, "Why do I have such a feeling?"), bring your attention back to feeling the sensations. *Feel. Feel. Feel.*

When you finally release the restrictions that inhibit you from feeling the full intensity of all the sensations, just sit with them for a short time.

If you are not attuned to your body, it might be challenging to allow yourself to feel. Remember, you are not looking for anything in particular. What you feel may be something very subtle. Again, honor all things equally. *Whatever* you feel, let your attention rest there.

Step Three: Developing Your Inner Vision

The next step we take is an important one, and a fun one as well. As you focus on the sensation, allow it to paint a visual interpretation for you to see in a form you can relate to. Your visual can be elaborate or simple. If you sit and watch the sensation, it might take the form of a Ferris wheel, a bag of sand, a heavy pipe, clouds, or dancing bears. It makes no difference; just feel and watch.

Sometimes I have a sensation but I can't find anything that describes it visually. I continue feeling it and say, "Is it this?" or "Is it that?" When I choose a visual that does not suit the sensation, my body rejects it. I can actually feel it being repelled. When I finally come up with a visual that accurately mirrors the sensation in my body, it beckons the visual to meld with it. This really happens and I find it amazing every time. When the visual is found, you can feel your body signal it is ready to go forward with the meditation. You have now begun the magical journey inward that silences your thinking and opens the doorway to your wisdom, or sixth sense.

You will notice that as your sensations change and move, so do your visuals. Notice that the more attention you give to the sensations, the more detailed they become. And the more detailed they become, the more movement and change you see. In short, you have become engaged in learning about *you*. As you move on, you will become more adept at observing the smallest nuance of your sensations, and with that comes an ability to see inside to the true natural energy called *you*.

Be patient and stay focused on the inner show. For now, you do not want to alter your body with deep breaths, for we are very much interested in observing the body as it is and letting it be your guide.

Recognizing the Origin of Sensation

The body has much to teach us if we take the time to learn its unique way of communicating. As you become more accustomed to feeling your body, you will learn to distinguish between the different types of sensations. You will become familiar with the multitude of emotion-related symptoms and the sensations associated with them. You will get so good at this that you will be able to recognize the emotional origin of all sensations.

What I mean by "recognize the origin" is this: Thought creates most of the sensations in the body, the Ego incarcerates the thoughts, and the body must endure the sensations until the Ego becomes weary of one drama and chooses to create another.

For example, you may recognize a sensation you feel in your body as tension arising from fear. That fear is generated by a thought that persists in your life. With that deduction you have found the origin of the sensation.

Feeling the sensation that the fear has created, rather than repeatedly recycling the content of the thought, will short-circuit the Ego's intent of keeping you focused on the fear.

Feeling the sensation that is created opens the doorway for something new and refreshing to take the place of the stagnant redundancy of thought.

Step Four: Adding Your Breath

Up to this point, we have not tried to alter anything about the body in its current state. As I earlier explained, that is on purpose and very important. Using the body as your guide for going inward is an essential part of creating a learning process that will function as a useful life tool.

Part of letting the body be as it is includes resisting the temptation to alter your breath pattern. After observing your body and acknowledging what information it has for you, you are ready to add to the process an element that will initiate change. You will observe the body in the same manner as before, but now you create movement by adding new breath patterns.

At first, take the tiniest of breaths by breathing in through your nose; notice everything about the breath. Feel the air passing through your nostrils. Does it feel cool? Can you feel your lungs expand? Now exhale through your mouth feeling the air passing over your lips. How does it feel? Does it feel cool as well, or not?

Allow yourself to take a slightly larger breath, and the next even larger. With each breath follow the breath in and out as before. Observe the feel of the air and how your lungs feel as they expand. Often at this stage I relish that deep breath and realize it has been a while since I have had a breath quite that satisfying.

Now take a breath that brings in all the air you can hold…one that fills up your chest cavity to the brim. Let your shoulders rise as you take in the last bit of air. Stop there and hold your breath just for one second before you exhale. Now relax and do nothing.

Step Five: Noticing Changes

Check your body again and notice any changes that occurred in the sensations you felt when you began. Take your time in using your Inner Vision to see/feel the difference. Be keen in your observations. Sometimes your mind will want to wander, and that is OK. But as soon as you find it out there in space, bring it back to the task at hand. Check out everything you feel and dismiss any content of thought. Luxuriate in your sensations by giving yourself permission to take your time.

Step Six: "Heave-Ho"

This next step just might surprise you. There is a preconception that if we are trying to learn to meditate, why would we do something that is expressive and loud? The reason is simple: We don't meditate to just be quiet and still. We meditate to learn. We learn best when the body is alive and flowing—that is its natural state. The movement I call "Heave-Ho" helps purge the body of any stuck or crimped energy patterns.

Begin slowly and gently. Inhale and then expel the air from your tummy by pumping the diaphragm with one quick heaving motion. This is similar to a cough, but not quite because a cough narrows off the air at the throat. In the Heave-Ho you propel all the air outward. Try it several times until the expelled air makes a rushing sound. Check yourself by placing one hand on your tummy and the other two inches from your mouth. When you make the movement, you should feel the tummy pulling abruptly inward while a blast of air hits your hand.

Now be brave and as you expel the air, make a rich and audible "Huh" sound…the louder, the better. Let the "Huh" sound come from deep in your body. Make the sound with your diaphragm, not your throat. You may have to try this several times to open your pathways so you can make a good, rich sound.

While the sound is fresh, feel the ripples of energy that you created in your chest. You may feel a variety of sensations: tingling, a rush of energy, or you may even feel a little light-headed. Do nothing at this time but observe the way you feel. Then do the "Huh" sound again, same as before. Can you feel the sensations and warmth you have created?

Make the "Huh" sound a couple more times and then do nothing but rest and allow your attention to focus on the stirring of energy that you have created.

Step Seven: Expanding Your Boundaries

An Interesting Phenomenon

In this step I bring to your attention a phenomenon I find extremely telling about how we create and hold stress in our bodies. It turns out that our Ego encourages us to hold on to or shut down our energy flow when there is a sudden change in the outer world. The Ego feels it is best to hold static or to restrain our energy when events stimulate emotional peaks and valleys. The Ego manages to confine our energy by creating the illusion that our bodies are impermeable containers. The illusion is designed to convince us that this new rush of energy cannot and must not escape. Subsequently, we feel the pressure of stagnant energy pressing outward against the imaginary walls.

If I were to speculate on why the Ego would choose such a tactic, I would say the Ego is using the technique of the animals in the wild when they remain motionless so as not to be seen. This is an excellent defense mechanism. But whatever the reasoning, this technique of survival is no longer necessary and not healthy for your body. And it no longer serves our purpose.

We will learn how to penetrate those illusionary boundaries and release the energy in this step.

When you need to bridge the gap between "I can't and I can," it is helpful to call on one of your most useful tools: your imagination. In this step I ask you to utilize this resourceful way of creating.

Returning to the meditation, once again perform the "Huh" sound. This time focus your attention on the sensations you created in your head. Here is where your imagination comes in.

Pretend you can see the boundaries of the sensations. When you can identify their outline, you will also see the shape. Let the sensations pulse or move in any and all directions, but continue to feel them until you can see their imaginary container. The idea of finding the shape should feel like a game, and not a difficult challenge. Using your imagination can make this fun. It does not have to be a shape you recognize; you just need to see it and its margins. I call this process Inner Vision. Take your time.

When you have identified your container of energy, remain focused on it for a few more seconds. Then gently take in a nice deep breath, and as you exhale imagine that you can expand the boundaries of the pretend vessel—the same kind of motion as if you were blowing up a balloon. With each breath let the boundaries continue moving outward. As it expands, let the boundaries dissolve into infinity. Imagine you can feel the energy escaping to freedom.

Do nothing but feel. You may only get a glimpse of the sensation having no boundaries. You may feel the spaciousness more than see it. And if you lose touch with the seamless sensation, you might choose to begin again. Any and all of what you experience is to be honored.

Step Eight: Adding Your Own Vibrations by Toning: The "Ahhh" Sound

You may already feel a release of tension or a sense of calm from what we have done so far, but when you add to the mix your own freshly created vibrations, you introduce something *very* innovative and *very* powerful; something from the present moment, something new, something untainted by design: *energy*. Adding your own vibrations enhances tenfold your experience of being in the present moment.

Start by making a tone using a soft "Ahhh." Some of you who sing might not have any problem with this, but those who don't may feel awkward. Be easy on yourself and know that you, too, can certainly do this. This is not about making a sound for others to hear, it is about creating vibrations. Make another "Ahhh." Focus solely on the feeling the sound makes in your body. Feel it in your chest, your throat, possibly in your head, or all of the above. Do not be concerned about how your "Ahhh" sounds. Feeling it, rather than hearing it, is the key.

Increase the volume of your next "Ahhh" so you feel its rumble in your chest. It doesn't take much added volume, just enough to feel the sound. I must emphasize, *feel* the sound. If your Ego jumps in and says your tones are not pleasing to the ear, let that not be of concern, just continue to *feel* the sound. Do not listen to the sound: *Feel* it. *Feel* it. *Feel* it.

Now feel the sensations as they move throughout your body and, as before, let your Inner Vision paint a picture of what you are feeling. This time you do not need to find the boundaries, but instead let your imagination find an image that suits the sensations. This is not to let your imagination run away with you but to enhance your involvement with the sensation.

Let your Inner Vision be your guide. The energy you create from toning naturally generates vibrations, which in turn creates a sensation of movement in the body. Allow your Inner Vision to follow that movement.

The word is *allow*. It is so important.

Allow your Inner Vision to create an image that depicts what your body is feeling: water surging, birds flapping, rubber bands pulling. Stay open to change because as you introduce more vibrations from the toning, the picture will change.

Make the "Ahhh" tone one more time.

Allow everything to develop in a freestyle manner. *All* is on the table. Let your imagination be expansive as you witness your inner stage.

Now take several deep breaths, placing your tongue at the roof of your mouth as you inhale through your nose and then exhale out your mouth.

Pause for a moment and take it all in.

Step Nine: The "Oh," "Oooh," and "Eee" Tones

Now make an "Oh" sound. In a couple of seconds, change it to an "Oooh" sound. Notice how the "Oh" sound feels and how you have to reform your lips to make an "Oooh" sound. Again, observe where you feel the vibrations in your mouth.

Notice you even feel the vibrations of the "Oh" sound in a different location in your body than the vibrations produced by the "Oooh" sound. But in order to feel the vibrations resonate in your body, make your tones as rich as they can be.

You may make the tones with any note. Be creative. You can change notes from one to the other. You can start high and go low. You can start soft and get louder. You can try any and all ideas that come to you.

Remember that the Ego will want to evaluate your sound, and I encourage you to sidestep it and move quickly on to examining in detail any sensation you detect from your toning. Take as long as you like in making these tones, but as soon as you have felt the vibrations in your throat or chest and have observed them several times you are ready to move on.

Now make an "Eee" sound, which creates a good deal of sensation. It is easier to create more volume with the "Eee" sound. Feel it rumble. Play with it as you make the sound. Move your lips and mouth to alter the sound. The intent is to feel and observe the inner visual, which will be filled with movement by now.

Pause for a bit to enjoy before we move on.

Step Ten: Moving Your Energy from Point A to Point B

You are now ready to take another step toward understanding your newfound abilities. Pretend that you can send the vibrations of the "Eee" sound out through your back. If you first pretend you can, you will see you *really* can.

Take a deep breath and as you make the "Eee" sound, visualize the vibrations penetrating through you and out of your back. Let your jaw drop open enough so you can make a full, strong "Eee." Let it resonate with a feeling of power so as to create a feeling of propelling yourself forward with the force. Do this several times. With an intense focus and strong vibrations, you will create a visual of fire or light coming out of your back. (I often feel a surge of energy when performing this part of the meditation.) If the Ego enters the stage, just return to feeling the vibrations. Let all your attention be directed to the wondrous sensations you are creating.

Pause and feel.

Step Eleven: Entering the SilentPlace

Take in a slow, deep breath through your nose, place your tongue at the roof of your mouth, and hold your breath for a count of three. Exhale through your mouth and hold your breath once again for three counts. In those three seconds, feel for a place within that is peaceful and generating warmth. Breathe gently and continue to feel that place of stillness. Use your inner eye and imagination to see a doorway or opening. (Sometimes I feel large doors opening and other times just a tiny area for me to move through.) Take one more deep breath, and as you exhale let it flow out through every pore of your body. See yourself gently slip inside the portal into your Soul space. This is what I call the SilentPlace. In this space, you allow *all* to be as it is. Feel and observe everything. This is your inner palace of wisdom. Seek nothing and allow all to come.

Sit in this sacred space for as long as you like. If your mind interrupts you more quickly than you wish, create another vibration by toning and bring your attention back to the sensations, rather than the thought.

Sit and relish what you have created for it is *yours—all yours.* The smallest of things are of significance. Each time you go inward you build upon your skills and refine your knowledge of how to be with the real *you.* The true, genuine *you* steps out of the shadows and reveals itself to the earthbound, Ego-controlled person you previously perceived yourself to be.

You are through.

I asked one of my students to describe how she felt while in the SilentPlace and she said the simple and profound words, "I feel holy."

I am not surprised, for that is truly what it is.

CHAPTER 15

A SAMPLE OF MY INNER JOURNEYS

To enhance your understanding of this process I'll share one of my own experiences. You will be able to follow me as I go on my inner journey. No two people are the same so it is a given that their journeys would not be either, but reading an account of mine might be helpful.

This example explains how I use Inner Vision Meditation as a tool for clearing away unwanted clutter from my head and reconnecting with my stronger, healthier, more productive self.

November 12, 2010

I made a decision this afternoon that I need meditation. I have had a morning filled with little fits and spurts of chaos, and I am now tense and no longer enjoying the day. The phone rings and when I answer, I notice the tone of my voice; it is not pleasant. The person on the other end presents me with another obstacle. This to me is a sure sign that I need a change in attitude. I can see that I am creating on the outside what I am feeling on the inside.

The biggest step I have to make is to stand up and announce to the others in my office that I will be gone for a bit, and I walk out the door. I find a spot where I can sit and be out of the flow of people and just out of earshot.

I think, "Too often I stop myself from taking necessary personal time by using the excuse that there is no place to be alone." I remind myself, "Close your eyes and you are alone."

When I close my eyes and begin the process of feeling my body, I am amazed at the intensity of the gyrations going on inside my head. I think, "How in the world did I let myself get in this shape?" I laugh at the thought because I recognize the critical voice of the Ego, and its judgment only adds to the drama.

I settle into my chair and turn my attention to focus solely on the sensations I feel in my head. At first the feeling is so scattered and rambunctious in an irritating way that I find myself not wanting to acknowledge it to the fullest.

I continue to do nothing but allow and feel. Then I add the task of visualizing what I am feeling. I sit, feel, and watch. In a minute or so, I am centered in the sensations, which are full of colors and lights, actually flashes of light—like thousands of flashbulbs going off.

In time I make the Heave-Ho "Huh" sound. I feel a rush of energy move through my body. I notice the change in my body. Before I made the "Huh" sound, I was unable to feel anything but my head. Now I am able to feel my chest.

I continue to focus on the sensations in my head but notice that they have changed. The activity in my head has become uniform. I can see a form to the sensation. It looks like a galaxy. I do nothing but watch for a period of time.

I add the toning of an "Eee" sound to create vibrations in my chest, and as I do, the galaxy turns into a swarm of bees. They seem to be frantic. I can feel the tightness from their fear of being trapped. They definitely want out. I continue to tone and a creative thought from the inside comes to me: "Open the windows, and let the bees fly free." I envision myself opening windows all around me. I can even see the curtains flowing with the fresh air that comes billowing inside. I add another soft "Eee" sound and let my attention return to the bees. I am amazed to see they have begun to arrange themselves into single-file formation. Around and around they go and then one by one they make their escape out the windows.

My head now feels empty and light. The feeling is blissful.

I sit and feel the clean, clear air moving through my head. I take one small breath and then a large one. I let my whole body surrender, and I feel the energy coursing throughout my body.

I begin to tone. I move through the "Ahhh," "Oooh," and "Eee" tones. I am alive with energy, and I feel pure and flowing.

I take several small breaths through my nose and out my mouth, and each breath amplifies the sensations in my body. Then I take a deep breath and hold it and exhale and hold it... there it is—the warm soft spot glowing near my heart. I know it to be the entrance to the SilentPlace. I slip inside and feel myself surrounded by expansive peace. It always amazes me that when I go through what seems to be a doorway into something, what I find is that I have gone outside to the seamless, timeless, expanse of the eternal Now.

I quietly relish the overwhelming feeling that all things are possible and a tear comes to my eye. The thought comes from deep with me: "Be gentle with yourself, you are still learning."

Another tear or two surfaces, but in no way are they tears of sadness—they are tears of profound gratitude.

I then have a wave of compassion for mankind. We are all still learning.

I know that I am through.

I open my eyes and observe how good I feel.

I am ready to return to work.

CHAPTER 16

MEDITATION IS A LIFELINE TO UNDER-STANDING HOW YOU FUNCTION

What you have just learned is more than a tool for quieting your mind. It is a lifeline to a fuller, happier life. It illuminates the pathway for creating choices where you once thought you had none. Inner Vision Meditation can change you from feeling like a lifeless puppet into a creative, spontaneous puppeteer.

Learning to identify the sensations in the body is the key to this liberation.

Anger, blame, sadness, resentment, irritability, fear, grief, along with a plethora of other emotions—they are common to us all. They certainly have their place as natural responses to adverse and difficult events in our lives.

(Notice I am talking about *you* and *your* emotions and responses and how *your* actions and reactions affect *you*. We are not evaluating anyone else's behavior. Linking your behavior to someone else's actions is an Ego trick to divert your learning process. Let others learn in their own time and in their own way.)

Emotions cease to be appropriate and no longer necessary when the heaviness of the feeling has hung on too long. They become obstructions to your happiness and health. There is a time to let all past emotions move on and make way for the new. Lingering emotions become attitudes. When emotions cease to be in flow and become mired in an Ego snare, they create forms of discomfort. They become stagnant and trap energy around them. They can cause a heavy ache deep inside the body or a feeling of being enveloped in a dark shroud. What began as a response to an outer occurrence can develop into lack of desire, loss of concentration, irritability, or depression. And the list goes on.

We all dislike these feelings but might not realize we have the ability to transform them into useful energy. All it takes is learning how to distinguish your thought processes from the sensations in your body.

One conscious effort to turn your attention to your body will sidetrack the thought. It is repeating the thought that creates the sensation. Feel the sensation and divert the thought.

This enables you to transform your emotions into something new and innovative and prepares you to exercise your right to let yourself be a healthy, happy human being. You do this by learning the art of letting go.

CHAPTER 17

THE ART OF LETTING GO

anoesis \an-oh-EE-sis\, noun: A state of mind consisting of pure sensation or emotion without cognitive content.

If you think about your Ego and how it messes with you, and magnify that by the amount of people there are on Earth, you can see where the turmoil of our world comes from.

Ranging from childhood to mere moments ago, you have bits of negativity that you choose to cling to. The choice to hang on to your Ego's rubbish or to let it go is yours. You have that choice in every moment of your life. Why choose to hang on to it? You only keep it around because you have become accustomed to how it feels. Even if it feels bad, you have adapted to the familiar garment of pain. The only garment you need is the garment of light.

Let go of the familiar rubbish and get ready to feel lighter and happier.

To let go you must first identify what you are holding on to. This isn't very hard; the old baggage shows up as a thought that often crosses your mind and is easy to identity because it never leaves you feeling good.

I touched on this earlier, but this time I approach it in a slightly different way. We start with a question: How was this reaper of havoc lodged in my world in the first place?

You can recall all too well the story that initiated the problem, but I want to show how that story managed to continue its involvement in your life for days, weeks, or even years later.

It goes like this: The Ego deems itself in charge of what is right or wrong for your well-being. It made these assessments from what it has experienced in the past. The Ego is its own judge and jury, so its opinion has never been challenged.

The moment the Ego identifies an act of infringement on its rules, it sends up red flags. When this happens you can feel the shudder run through your body. The alert has been sounded to protect an imaginary boundary line, which the Ego alone created. It built this illusionary boundary to protect your honor, your pride, and your name.

When that boundary is crossed and the Ego gets provoked, your *thinking* ability readily joins the cause. Now the

Ego has a partner and one that can help it verbalize its complaints.

If the Ego feels the infringement is severe enough, it will submit it for review repeatedly—as if one more time through the review process can change the outcome. Notice the event that caused the original feeling has long since come and gone. Each time you recount or review the subject, you re-create the uncomfortable feelings from the original moment. You feel the thrust of the original pain as if it had just happened. The Ego likes to chew on the past like a dog with a bone, and keeps the emotion captive by repeating the thought process.

The negative feeling in the body would dissipate if you were not asked by the Ego to rehash the event in your head. In order to keep the emotion restricted, a force field or constriction is placed around it. It will not be able to leave until you break the *thinking* cycle. Each time you replay the negative thought, you put an additional layer of restricted energy in place. The only way to break this cycle is to *feel* rather than think. When the cycle is broken, even for a few seconds, you have a precious opening to experience yourself without the burden of the old emotion. The next thought can be one of joy. When you turn your attention to *feeling* rather than *thinking*, you make space for something new to enter… space for a moment of creativity.

When your thoughts change, so does your life.

Learning to utilize this tool helps you observe the Ego in your daily activities. But in order to see, feel, and believe that the Ego is illusionary you must find your way inward to the Soul, where the Ego is not in charge. You cannot alter the Ego's behavior while playing in its sandbox. You cannot solve any problem while engulfed in its negativity.

You know it is time to go inward when you are in need of fresh, healthy thoughts, which will, without fail, produce fresh, healthy ideas for a fresh, healthy life.

We do this by utilizing what we have learned…by feeling the Ego's clinched fist.

Being in touch with feeling versus thinking is the way to be in the Now. The Now holds no fear, so in that moment the Ego feels safe and ceases signaling to rethink the old. This is when you see that fretting is not a productive way to spend your time. Breathing with the Now and letting things flow feels good and can become your new feeling of choice. We would, of course, all like to stay in the state of bliss but that is not how we learn. We learn by allowing ourselves to experience life, and when we find ourselves stuck in the viscous thoughts of the Ego, we can tell by the way we feel that it is time once again to purge ourselves of the unwanted.

Let it *all* go.

When the energy is freed, the discomfort is gone and a gift of understanding and compassion take its place. The situation has not changed, but your attitude toward it has.

You will find that when your attitude changes, so do your surroundings.

I enter most meditations with no agenda and I don't always do the exact same things. But if there is an obvious obstruction standing in the way of happiness, I enter into the meditation knowing there is work to be done, and can only be done by feeling my way through the choppy waters.

When you are in touch with your sensations, you have the unique benefit of being able to view your thoughts and feelings from a different vantage point.

One by one, go through the process of letting them go. See your grip on them loosen. Actually see your hand let go. See them as balloons or birds that you set free, but *see* it. Be deliberate in your intent to *feel* the release.

You may come upon something that you can't seem to release. This issue is the one that will lead you to your biggest lessons. And once released, the wisdom of that lesson will be revealed to you. When you feel resistance to letting it go, ask yourself the hard question: "What will I lose if I let it go?" but continue to return to the sensation. If you return to the feeling of constraints, the information that comes to you will be from your inner wisdom and not from your Ego. This is a magical feeling and it happens. It really does!

Don't *try* to let go, as that puts you at odds with the Ego. Visualize the sensation of tension as a gripped first, a bundle of tied knots, or two men clashing in a fierce battle. Let the visual suit the sensation. You will be amazed at what your intuition can create to show you the depth of your emotions. Continue breathing and toning into the sensation and let it become free of boundaries.

The breath and vibrations from toning naturally introduce the idea of expansion, and this in turn initiates the loosening and undoing of the antagonistic combative feeling. You will notice that negative energy wants to pull inward while positive energy wants to flow outward. As you allow yourself to be absorbed by your animated sensations, the visuals will change. Although you do not have your mind engaged at this time, the Ego is observing what your inner truth is doing with its important earthly problem.

You have released most of the Ego's influence, but there is that one thread that is hard to release. Here is where you learn about *you*.

The Ego is holding on to the problem and not *you*. Using your now elevated sensory perception, feel the energy that is required to service the Ego's notion of what is important. Feel how it is energetically attached.

If it is fear you are working with, you may feel the energy is frantically trying not to miss something important. If it is guilt, you may see the Ego frantically trying to hide. Each visual scenario tells the story you need to hear. See it and feel it.

If you can stay engrossed in observing, you soon see that the activity begins to lessen. Whether it is your Soul's wisdom or source, the comforting sensation of trust slips its way in and the Ego senses that there is no need for fretting.

Ah, the wondrous feeling of surrendering the sword is at hand.

With grace and ease the release is made. The energy is set free. Sometimes I feel a rush move through me, sometimes I cry for joy, but I always come back from the meditation a happier, wiser person. Making a healthy choice is your next natural inclination.

The Ten Steps to Letting Go

Step One	Realize you have something that needs to be released.
Step Two	Sit in your favorite spot, pick up your crystals or symbolic objects, and close your eyes.
Step Three	Feel the sensations in your body.
Step Four	Focus on the feeling…let it become visual.
Step Five	Use breathing and toning to amplify the sensations.
Step Six	Follow the inner show.
Step Seven	Trust in what you see.
Step Eight	Let your breath assist you in expanding the sensations.
Step Nine	Continue observing the sensations as they transform.
Step Ten	Listen to your inner wisdom.

The following is a transcription of one my own personal meditations. Reading an actual account of this technique will help you see more clearly how this process unfolds.

April 11, 2011

I awaken in the morning and before I can blink the second time, my Ego begins racing about trying to locate and reconstruct a situation that occurred the previous day. The situation has obviously left my Ego with negative feelings and it has decided I need to rehash it one more time.

(This kind of repetitive negative thinking is always a sign that I need to let something go. It also tells me that my morning meditation has a gift waiting for me.)

I toss around the idea of whether or not I want to follow my usual morning routine with my meditation coming after I eat breakfast or if I should go straight to my sitting chair. I resolve the question by noticing that I am hungry and do not want anything to distract me from my core purpose. A cup of tea and yogurt later and I am in my chair.

I light a candle and hit my Tibetan bowl and feel its soothing vibrations. Then I place my favorite crystals in my hands.

When I turn my attention to sensing my body, it is not hard to pull away from the distracting commotion of thoughts. As usual I begin to focus on the feelings the action is creating, not the content of the thoughts. The activity is intense and produces a sick, heavy feeling. That yuck is hard to focus on. I feel repelled by it and wonder for a split second what I should do next. I quickly catch the emotion as being another diversionary tactic of the Ego and remember all I need to do is feel and observe— and that is what I do. After watching the far-flung action that the thoughts cause for a little while, I move a little closer to the revolting, heavy feeling. I am ready to give the "Heave-Ho" now. I have the sensations in my sights. The "Huh" sound I make startles me; it sounds almost animal-like. I know to bring my attention back to the sensations and not let judgment of the Ego hijack the meditation. I make the "Huh" sound again, and this time the energy that I create gushes forward and out of my body. I am shocked that I can create so much energy that quickly.

Surrounded now with energy flying everywhere, I begin to let myself tune into my inner screen. The rambunctious goings-on immediately turn into a large tribe of enraged native people performing an intense war dance. I sit there and watch for the longest time. Then it occurs to me to see if I can feel the beat of the drums. As I follow the sensations, I can feel myself move lower and deeper into my chest and into my heart area. It comes to me that the tribe is trying to protect my heart. As I begin to approach my heart area, I can feel their moves become more hostile.

It is then that I introduce several small breaths…and a light hum. I need to keep my hum soft so as not to excite them any more than need be. With the humming comes a sense that I can get closer to the action.

I allow myself to make the soft "Oh" sound and then an "Oooh." Each sound helps me move closer to my heart. As the sensations grow so does the visual...I can see that one of the tribe is obviously the chief. I can hear clearly the drumbeat now. I then feel my heart be the drumbeat. I am creating the rhythm for their dance. My heart becomes a medicine man–type character, who emerges carrying the drum of my heart. He waves his hand for the rest of the tribe to take their places at his feet. Without words, he seems to be saying, "Now what is the problem here?" He mesmerizes almost all of the tribe, but there is one member who is still agitated and frightened. The medicine man seems to know that he has to let the young native touch and hold the drum to prove that all is well. Without words the medicine man communicates to the tribe that the drum will make the rhythmic beat without even striking it and that it is eternally protected and powerful, and they have nothing to fear. All is well. The tribe gives a sigh of relief and my body lets go... of all of its tension and releases new energy back into the space that was emptied.

I am deeply moved by what I witness. My swirling energy creates this tale and I feel that if I sit quietly it will continue to unfold in front of me. I sense a powerful lesson working its way upward and it will soon surface into my awareness. The imaginary medicine man I have manifested is in sync with my anticipation of more. He looks straight at me and then with a nod, he turns to the warriors and begins to communicate with them. He does so without speaking, but his thoughts are clear to me. He wants them to tell him why they have been so afraid. He wants to know if they are in fear of losing their lives. All without words they say, "No…not our lives…our honor."

With this, I can feel the tears begin to well up in my eyes as I make the connection of what I was hearing with what had occurred to me the previous day. But my desire to see and learn more is stronger than all other desires. I can feel the story line developing and don't want to miss anything. My energy keeps surging and my inner creativity for learning keeps giving. The story continues.

It seems that the day before, this group had separated itself from the main tribe while out hunting. This was not forbidden, but it was understood that if the choice was made, it was very important to stay alert to the body's good senses.

Shortly after they had chosen to leave the others, the warriors came upon the perfect hunter's catch. Their adrenaline surged as they ran to overtake their prey. The chase was intense and filled with sordid emotions. Not being attuned to their surroundings as they normally were caused them to stray beyond familiar territory, and to their surprise, they met another tribe.

It was customary for the group to look to their chieftain for a sign indicating whether the tribe was friend or foe, but the warriors had strayed too far from his helping hand. Their good senses had been overtaken by the passion of their chase. When they looked for their senses to guide them in this moment, all they could feel was the tightness in their chests, which were filled with uncertainty and fear. They had lost touch with their good senses and let their defenses take control.

Thankfully before anyone was hurt, the chieftain from the other tribe showed them the sign of peace. There was a moment of tense silence as both sides tried to gather themselves, then the other chieftain motioned with his hands the direction the warriors needed to travel to return to their tribe.

The separated tribe feared their lack of appropriateness and absence of judgment had reflected badly upon their tribe's good name. It was greatly feared that their actions would bring forth the ancient curse of the gods. The lore was that if a clansman brings shame upon the tribe, it would cause the sacred tribal heart to stop beating.

Again, I did not hear, but felt the words tumbling out of the medicine man, "The lesson has been learned. When our senses are lost to us, we, too, are lost. No matter how intense the moment, we must stay attuned to our surroundings and others. Now, be grateful for the next breath you take, for it will be the breath of forgiveness. It will cleanse you of the past and place you in the arms of a new beginning. Know that the lessons you learn write the words for the songs that teach your children. Now lay down your swords and sing brave warriors. Sing."

A smile comes over me as I remember the words, "Sing, brave warrior, sing." They came from one of my all-time favor-

ite CDs, Heart Land, *by Tim Wheater, music that brings me to tears every single time I hear it.*

Then I heard myself say in a soft voice, "With every breath you are brand-new." And then I say, "You are forgiven." The tears start streaming down my face and they are tears of joy... the joy of knowing the richness of forgiveness.

I sit for a while just breathing and feeling...feeling how good it feels to feel joy coursing through my body and how grateful I am to know how to do this work.

This process took seventeen minutes.

CHAPTER 18

IMPROVING YOUR ABILITY TO VISUALIZE

As you work with Inner Vision Meditation, you will become better and freer with visualizing your sensations. Every day there is something new. You may encounter a new sensation or have the same sensation as yesterday, but there will be something about the visualization that is different. No two moments in time are alike. The inner movie you view is always different. It is the premiere and you have the front-row seat. It doesn't take drama in your life to accumulate unwanted, stagnant debris. Just being human and functioning on this planet stirs up emotions that we have yet to learn how to readily transform. As you begin your daily meditation, know that you are about to let your wisdom's imagination guide you to the place of learning and growing. Your higher self's imagination will have fun conjuring up new visuals for you. Visualizations do not need to be lengthy or in as much detail as the previous example to be helpful. They can be brief glimpses, yet empowering. Here is what I mean:

One day I felt tightness in my body. When I began my meditation, I surprised myself when the following image came to me:

I am surrounded by rolls of carpet. I chuckle to myself. "Carpet?" But my attention goes back to the sensation and I continue. The rolls of carpet are huge and close to me. They have me hemmed in. It feels terribly confining and is causing a slight, but noticeably anxious, feeling. Going through the process of sensing sensations and doing my deep breathing, I feel the surge of energy. With one exhale comes the idea to give the carpet rolls an energetic shove. With a heartfelt "Heave-Ho" exhale, I give a big imaginary push and send the carpets tumbling away. The tightly coiled bundles flow outward and become inviting runways of opportunities.

This visualization created a wonderful sensation of letting go.

Another example from times when I felt heaviness in my chest:

A variety of ball images…bowling balls, beach balls, and soccer balls.

But it is always the sensation that commands which type, size, and color I see.

I usually try giving the balls a toss. If that does not feel right, I try rolling them away or simply putting them down on the ground. I work with the sensation until I find what feels right. Once I have found the method that best suits my situation, I complete the release and wait for the new energy to enter. It is always such a welcome relief to be in the presence of a fresh, new me. You will see how creative you really are when you allow yourself to see who you really are. Inner Vision Meditation is your most useful tool for unveiling and revealing concepts that are profoundly clear and useful in your life. Staying current with yourself is so very important. You can drift away so quickly, but when you make it a daily ritual or habit (like brushing your teeth) to sit and feel through your body, you will amaze yourself and others with your ability to see to the truths of situations. All it takes…*all* is takes, is the time to sit.

CHAPTER 19

MORE THAN YOU THOUGHT
POSSIBLE

Inner Vision Meditation is an amazing way to learn. Not only do you become at one with your own inner strengths and core beliefs, but you also find yourself on the same vibrational frequency as the universe. It is as if you can speak its language. You can be shown and understand the most meaningful intricacies, or get a glimpse of and comprehend the grand laws of the universe. When you go inward what you see is not always just about you; it can be lessons that encompass everyone and everything.

It can also depict for you a new way of understanding something that is simple in your mind but elusive when you try to describe it. I am grateful when I am shown visual presentations of new ways to explain my teachings to my students. They are often cartoonlike, and can make me blurt out laughing. This sounds odd for a meditation, but it is true, and I love it when it happens. Nonetheless, I find the allegories priceless and they help me put my thoughts in a framework that is easier to grasp. The concepts I teach can be foreign to our antiquated thinking. My ideas can seem obtuse to the thinking part of your brain. If the thinking side of us doesn't understand something, it will gloss over it and miss out on the wisdom that the new ideas hold. Animated cartoons may be just the thing your mind needs to be more receptive to new philosophies.

What follows is a great example of what I am talking about:

Deep in meditation I found myself basking in that remarkable feeling of having no constraints and being unencumbered. The meditation was drawing to a close and I felt complete. My attention was then drawn to a sensation. I began to focus on it and let it develop into an image. I remember the thought crossing through said, "My, this is late in the meditation to be seeing so much activity." It was a full-blown skit-like enactment.

I saw my Soul self, a seamless stream of consciousness, making the conscious decision that it was time to reenter the body. It was making this beautiful mist-like movement toward my crown chakra. Without being said, it was unmistakably clear that my Soul was showing me how important returning to the body is. The Soul had to don the physical body when it returned to the earth dimension in order to be seen. That got a big laugh out of me. The thought of the body being necessary apparel had not occurred to me.

But the story doesn't end there; the scene became more elaborate. The idea of putting the body on as a garment began to expand. Instead of one choice of attire, I saw an entire wardrobe room with masks, crowns, flowing dresses, suits of armor, you name it. Still feeling the smooth, graceful energy of the Soul, I could see her choice of attire would be a flowing dress or something comfortable and soft.

But what happened next captivated me. I could see/feel the Ego presence moving in and getting closer. As I watched I wondered what was coming next, I heard the Ego say, "Hey, you didn't ask me if you could wear that. Remember, you're on my turf now." The Ego had no defined shape or size; it was more of a presence than an object. But I could feel its uneasiness as if it felt its job security was threatened. I could feel the Ego luring me into its vibrational field. It began searching through my past for a piece of guilt or fear to bring up and wave in front of me, which was intended to let me know that I needed it for protection.

The Ego attached the dormant negativity to a vibration, the vibration manifested into a thought, and the thought became an emotion—just as the Ego had planned. Then the Ego went to work determining what type of protection I would need to ward off those nasty demons from the past.

Next thing I knew, my desire for the flowing dress was gone and I had on a flak jacket and heavy mukluks on my feet. Then the jacket turned into Harry Potter's invisible cloak and I had on a heavy necklace around my neck. I know this because I could feel it pressing against my heart.

I thought to myself how amazing it was that as the outfits changed so did my emotions, and then following suit, so did my body. Next the imaginary garb disappeared and I sat there feeling the residual effects of the Ego's charade. As it dwindled away, I realized how the wardrobe room loomed closely to the surface of my day-to-day life, and what the Ego chose for me affected how I interacted with my surroundings.

I stopped as that insight crossed my radar screen. I stopped and gave a deep "Heave-Ho." I quickly felt the Soul's mist surround me and knew my inner strength was still present. I felt *choice* return as my champion. I felt light and free. Free to be. Comfortable in my own skin with no need or want for more.

As I reflected on this Inner Vision Meditation lesson, I saw the depth of its teaching. I had become aware of the make-believe ensembles and I could feel them when they were in place. I could tell that sometimes I felt like I woke up already wearing one. If the Ego determines I need to have protection or teach me a lesson, it will fit me in the finest attire. Additionally, there is the veil of protection used for shielding me from the pain of being rejected. And, there is the dense shroud of protection to keep me from falling in love and running the risk of a broken heart. There is also the frightfully too-heavy robe of grief, which the Ego deems necessary and is painfully difficult to shed. And there is the annoying little Miss-Goody-Two-Shoes outfit that gets put on many women early in life so as to never fall out of favor with anyone. I can't say I know what that one feels like, but I sure have met some of these women in my travels.

You can see this analogy could go on forever. Whatever your fears or shortcomings, your Ego has something in its closet to make sure no one ever sees the blemish in your character. It has something for every dark moment, but not a thing for a moment of bliss. The idea has never occurred to the Ego to let your uniqueness shine or that your oddities are your untapped resources for joy and success in life.

The part of this curious tale to heed is how intense these feelings, these trappings, can feel. If fresh, clear, energy enters into your body after a meditation and the Ego jumps in to throw a horsehair serape around you for protection from who knows what, you will feel it right away, don't you think?

You laugh, but that is exactly how the Ego works, and I want you to see it and feel it. Until you can actually feel the effects of the Ego, you will not be able to catch it in action. To teach anything a new behavior you must catch it in the act: dog, kids, and Ego, all the same.

More important, realize that you have a choice. The Ego is not your wardrobe director. This is hard to fathom since you've been at its mercy all these years, but you can slip out of that heavy sad-sack dress into something light and comfy and have the Ego go do something productive—to leave you to *be* for a while.

I do not call this a lesson so much as a realization. It was amazing to realize how different my body felt from one day to the next. I saw how the feelings of my body correlated with the attitude or outlook I had that day. I had fun visualizing what kind of outfit it felt like I was wearing, and if the outfit fit the attitude as well. This sort of playful observation opens expansive avenues of self-discovery.

Inner Vision Meditation can lead you through the steps of making a wardrobe change for your body. As the body sheds its stuck energy, it also sheds the sensation of feeling confined. Free-flowing energy makes for a happier body and a happier you.

Outside Interference Feels Like the Real Thing

Sometimes your body can feel an emotion that is not induced by thought. The body can ingest or come into contact with a substance or be deprived of something essential, which can cause the body to exhibit the same sensations as if you were angry or sad. For instance, if you have one cup of coffee too many in the morning your body responds in kind. You are aware that your body feels differently, but what you are not aware of is that your body has taken on an aggressive posture…racing heartbeat, clinched jaw, and hyperawareness.

The signals are sent out and your body is placed on alert. It is prepared for a fight when there is no enemy in sight. If you are not careful, the next person you encounter might see a less than pleasant side of you. The ingestion of one cup too many precipitated the change in your body, but it wasn't the coffee that made you irritable. It was the way the caffeine made your body feel. That irritating, clamped feeling makes you react negatively. You can get it from too much caffeine, too much pain medication, or from holding on to a grudge, but still it is the body that tells you things are not right.

Sometimes you have to say to yourself "That is the coffee talking," or "It's the lack of sleep talking," and take a comforting, deep breath, knowing that the real you will return shortly. But being aware that you feel tightness in your body and especially in the face or jaw can help you avoid many of those unpleasant "unlike you" moments.

So whether or not you are hungry or have taken an antihistamine that has left your body feeling different from normal, being a good body listener always works to your advantage. When you know your body, you know yourself.

CHAPTER 20

GRAVITY ∞ MOVEMENT ∞ SHAPE OF ROUND

As you progress you will feel your senses become heightened. You will notice the smallest of things in your body, things that you have ignored or not even detected in the past. This keen sense is a sacred tool to be cherished and utilized. You will be amazed at how the authentic *you* will surface and how your *truth* will become your most valuable possession.

But what you learn goes beyond the boundaries of your body. During the process of moving inward to your Silent-Place and while you rest in that space of just being, you are learning. You are learning from your senses about the matrix of the universe. You can see that as you learn about your own intricacies of evolving, you learn how all things evolve. The best way to describe this is to say: Your visuals will utilize the universe's most basic components of truths for its illustrations. It is not so much the initial visual that shares this precious piece of wisdom, but the manner of transformation and the end result. With a quieted mind, an open heart, and a willingness to be a dedicated observer, you will find that you have embarked on knowledge that ranges from the teachings of quantum physics to the secrets of the ancient mystery schools.

This is a taste of what I am talking about.

When you begin meditations and go about the process of visualizing your sensations, you will often come across the feeling of something stationary and linear, like a yoke that runs across your shoulders or a shaft that seems to extend from your head to your sternum. The differences in the images are endless, but the significance of the vision is always powerfully the same. During our daily activities, the Ego manages to go unnoticed as its less than supportive attitudes and unnecessary criticisms cause tension in our bodies. This tension creates restrictions, which block our body from its natural flow. As the moving energy encounters these constricted areas, the flow becomes congested and ultimately clogged. This forms an invisible yet undeniably uncomfortable sensation in your body. When my students describe this sensation in visual terms, they often refer to it as something linear, such as a stick, pole, or pipe. When asked to describe this sensation, they will say the mass feels heavy, it has sharp edges, and feels stuck.

From observing this same mass in myself, I have learned the most effective way to transform its heaviness is to let it do what it naturally wants to. I learned this by carefully observing my inner visual of it and feeling its slightest tendencies. For instance, I noticed that the heaviness of the object made me want to droop from its weight. It created a downward-pulling sensation…downward, downward toward Earth. I took that cue and with my breathing began to lower it to where it seemed to want to go. Each time I found a different way to do this.

Once I saw the form tied in place by strings, so I loosened the strings and lowered it to the ground.

Another time I saw a big, burly man holding a barbell to his chest. I could see his arms in a tightly curled position, and the strain on his face told me he was struggling to maintain this posture. When I suggested it was no longer necessary for him to support this large cumbersome weight and that if he wished he could lay it down, his face changed from anxiety to relief.

These took place in slow motion as I was toning and using the vibrations in my body to create energy of movement and strength. In each of these instances and others like them, I have found that when I feel the weight touch the ground and I am no longer resisting gravity, I feel a burst of energy as it begins to flow once again. When I feel its movement the first thing I feel is the edges of the mass begin to soften and before long the energy is swirling in a galaxy-like spiral. It is round.

This sounds so incredibly simple, but the shape of round is the elementary shape of all things that exist…from spinning quarks to massive galaxies. Another obvious detail that becomes apparent when observing this phenomenal transformation is that *nothing* exits without movement. It is no coincidence that quantum physicists have determined that everything that exists in the universe is in motion.

When the Ego tries to wrangle energy into a confined area, the body feels tight, repressed, and wrong. Your body knows that confining energy is unnatural. It tells you that the Ego has stepped in and created an unhealthy situation. It is not only your job, but your calling, to learn when this has occurred and come to your body's rescue. Your goal is to not let the body stay in this unnatural state for an extended length of time. Flowing energy is vital to your health, affects how you feel physically, and how you feel about our surroundings.

I take this one step further. When you feel the energy release in your body, you return to being in sync with the universe or the *All* or God. It is time we see how important our existence is to the whole. It is time for humankind to see they are a microcosm of the whole. We, like all things, are a fractal. The smallest molecule in us represents the whole universe. We, and our energy, are important to all that exists.

We are in the process of evolution along with the elements of the universe. It is the way of all things.

Our part is not only to believe this, but also to *feel* this. Feeling will cause you to believe it. Each time you go inside and feel how life is real to the touch, you realize you are much more than the chatter in your head. But even more incredible is that you see and feel how *you*—the *true you*—can weave your energy into powerful tools of manifestation. Free and flowing energy creates free and flowing energy. Only the Ego can interrupt the flow, and now you know how to alter that.

CHAPTER 21

USING WHAT YOU HAVE LEARNED

When you have learned to feel and identify clearly the times the Ego is at work in your life, you can turn to Inner Vision Meditation to learn the life lesson before you. Staying in touch with your current sensations can lead you through simple visual depictions of how it feels to have the Ego's veil over your eyes. By observing the inner visuals that your sensations create, you can gain insights that not only transform you in that moment, but are profoundly important to your karmic evolution.

This is when you can use the meditation practice to not only be a method of releasing and letting go of unwanted tension, but also as an irreplaceable tool for spiritual growth.

You only need to be open to allowing your inner visual world to unfold for you. As you feel, you see the transformation of your life lessons as inner pictorial messages. It is important to continue to add the breath and toning to the scenes so that new energy can be introduced to the situation.

What may start as a visual of heaviness and darkness becomes a sumo wrestler. As you breathe and tone, he ceases to be so large or so intent on wrestling. He may disappear completely and be replaced by a dove sitting on a nest of eggs. Your interpretation of these images is not of importance. What is important is to see how differently you feel when you have converted stuck energy to soft, free willingness. It is later that the meaning of your meditation will be revealed to you. To engage the thought process to figure it out is a return to the old habit of trying to think through every detail of things to decipher meaning. That is a trap from the Ego and bars you from being in touch with senses. It is through your senses that the universe speaks to you.

Your skill using your senses in any given moment can guide you to learning things about yourself that you have never seen before. The reason you're able to see things more clearly is that when you observe yourself from this inner perspective, you see things more loosely woven. What might have appeared to be a tightly bound ball of yarn before your time in meditation has now become a spacious area that encompasses strands of yarn and free, empty space. You can view one strand at a time and see each strand's beginning and end. This feeling of inner spaciousness is essential to seeing certain aspects of your life from different angles. Instead of dissecting or picking something apart with your intellect, you are able to see not only the whole picture, but also the parts that make up the *whole*. With your imagination, you can stand back, circle it, or go inside, and in so doing, you can *know* what makes you tick. It provides a nonthreatening environment for honesty to flourish.

It was during a meditation not too long ago that this ability to view myself from a clutter-free room revealed a very interesting concept that I could see applied to more than just me:

I was sitting in the peace of the SilentPlace and nearing the end of my meditation. I had some life situations that had been bothering me before the meditation. So I decided to review one previous thought-of-as-negative circumstance, and see and feel how I would respond now that I was not in an Ego-driven environment.

In this particular meditation, I saw the Ego's antics off to the side as I brought the situation forward. My body was no longer reacting to the Ego's gestures for attention. It felt empowering to have this once confounding situation not have control over me.

Since I was feeling unaffected by what I had once thought of as a dilemma, I chose to view another situation that my Ego had earlier deemed problematic. This second situation was a different type of concern, but I noticed that the Ego's antics of revulsion were the same. At that time I just made note of my observation. But later I led myself through a more intensive discovery. To my amazement there was a theme that ran through my Ego's repertoire of dislikes. Whether it was dreading the idea of emptying the dishwasher or fretting over something it thought was unjust in the world, it had the same underlying signature singsong attitude.

Same Slant, same Attitude, same Tone. I asked my husband to come up with a word combining all the words and he quickly said, "Slatatone." It stuck. There are exceptions to this observation, but most of time the Ego is in its Slatatone posture. You will be amazed how pervasive its Slatatone is in your life.

Find your Slatatone and how your Ego colors your world when you let it do the painting. Do a scan of your body to see. Is your Ego in charge of you, or are you the master of your being? It is not always easy to make the shift, but knowing that your earthy self is currently inhabited by the Ego's drive will help you find your desire to return to balance.

Know that we are not in search of being without the Ego's fits and spurts. We are not seeking perfection. Trying to become flawless is a trap. Our aim is to recognize that we have choices, and knowing what our choices are. From being able to assess one's self objectively, we learn to feel where we need to alter our approach to life's challenges.

We learn to observe our fiery Ego's activities and determine which parts of its actions are beneficial and which are not. We learn to feel when we have become veiled and shut down, and are able to recognize the sense of emptiness that looms in the place of joy. We learn to know when it feels right to say, "I am sorry," and welcome the feeling of warmth that forgiveness brings. We learn to feel when it feels right to stand up for ourselves and speak our mind. We learn to stand behind, beside, but never in front of our true selves.

We learn all of this by feeling. When it feels wrong in our bodies it *is* wrong. When it feels right in our bodies it *is* right…right for you.

CHAPTER 22

FEEL THE CREATIVE GENIUS INSIDE

Once you have tapped into this magical inner space, you have at your fingertips many wondrous tools, and among them is your creative genius. Although it is a magical place, it is not the magic performed by sleight of hand. Your creative ideas may feel like they come out of thin air, but indeed they are grounded in truth. To fathom this phenomenon and see its validity, I use an analogy that you might be familiar with.

I call it "shower knowledge." Others have experienced this, but if you have not, once I describe it you will recognize something in your life that is similar. Shower knowledge is just that—when I am in the shower I get clear ideas about all kinds of things: from glorious inspiration to basic clarity, or a solution to a problem that has me stumped.

Why does your creative genius decide to come forth while in the shower? The reason is very simple, and also explains why Inner Vision Meditation is so effective. As the hot water tumbles across your body, your complete attention is drawn to the sensation the water creates when it hits your skin. Everyone has what they feel is the perfect temperature for the water, and when that is reached your total being is enveloped in the warmth. If you, in that moment, yield and allow the sensations to overtake you, you are rewarded with the wonderful feeling of surrendering. At that moment all the cells open and it's out with the old and in with the new.

The act of directing your attention to the feeling of the water on your body triggers the release of tension, and the natural result of flowing energy is creation. Being in the center of sensation is the spawning ground for creativity. You might have this while running or planting spring flowers, but the key is surrendering to the moment and making space for creativity to flourish.

I would not have seen how this all works if I had not observed it in my meditations. Many times I have gone into a meditation with a portion of my body blocked in some way. Once I have followed the steps of honoring it, feeling it, seeing it, and toning vibrational waves of change through it, I find myself humbly surrendered to that moment. In this energized moment of silence, I am often given a nugget of wisdom. It could be an inspired and clever idea, how to build something, or a simple statement of fact that opens my eyes to something I had never known before…I hear or see—or both!—a universal truth.

Sometimes I am shown pieces of a life puzzle that are obscured from my Ego's vision, but when they are seen from the Soul's perspective, they reveal the whole picture. Other times I am shown how to illustrate or explain something very meaningful to me and to others. I do not go into a meditation in search of these treasures. That would be entering a meditation with the Ego leading the way.

Not every meditation brings forth a gift of wisdom, but they all evoke a feeling of being refreshed, clear-minded, and pure of heart.

I love the times that I learn something about myself and how the Ego is operating in my life. I am always spellbound when I realize that I have the tool to feel and see the clinched fist of the Ego as it desperately hangs on to its shield in an effort to dodge the blows of being wrong.

These meditations bring about insight and change, and I find they repeatedly remind me how valuable this technique is to living a fulfilled life. I am always humbled when I find that, as in so many times before, I can follow the gripped sensation inward and see in living color what being wrong actually represents to the Ego. This visual is extraordinarily telling in and of itself, but I know that the true gift comes when this energy is transformed. I know that by staying attuned to my inner vision and infusing my vibrations into the stuck energy, change will occur. This change is inevitably felt as a loosening of the grip.

I breathe and watch in awe as the lesson manifests itself right in front of me. I see displayed for me all I need to know to initiate change. Then I sit in heartfelt appreciation of this incredible method I have found. It is truly a sacred, magical way of spiritually evolving. When I finish a meditation, I know in the deepest part of my being that I am learning to be a valuable participant in the evolution of humanity.

How to do this has been laid out for you, but what *you* must add is your willingness to try and to be trusting of yourself. You must learn to utilize your ability. You must be creative and inventive. You do that by allowing yourself to be free and spontaneous.

Wisdom comes through the imagination. Some would say, "That means you are just making it up."

I say, "An imagination that has no boundaries, blossoms into a creative genius."

We all have our own creative genius waiting to bloom. When we are creating, we are in the flow of *all* creation… we can feel our inner worth…we can feel our strength…we know ourselves inside and out. We not only know, but *feel* the meaning of love. We are Love.

It is yours to behold. It is pure. It is real.

ABOUT THE AUTHOR

Beth Johnson is a native Texan and graduate of the University of Houston. She has practiced meditation since 1980 and began teaching her own technique called Inner Vision Meditation in 1994. She is the author of two other books on meditation. *First You Sigh* tells how Beth came to meditation as a way of life, and presents an easy to follow guide for the beginner; *Thoughts From the Inside* is a selection of poignant thoughts influenced by years of mediation practice. In her new book, *Coming to Your Senses*, she shares the awe-inspiring gifts of Inner Vision Meditation.

Beth and her husband own a ranch near Sisterdale in the Texas Hill Country. She raises horses; runs a Bed, Breakfast and Barn; teaches meditation and shares the insights she has learned from her Inner Vision meditation. Her passion is the

Silent Place Temple. She built it to overlook the horse arena and all guests are invited to go inside to spend some valuable quiet time.

Beth's website is www.silentplace.com, and SisterCreek Ranch's website is www.sistercreekranch.com.

KIRKUS
REVIEWS

Johnson's (*First You Sigh*, 2000) sound, well-paced self-help book on meditation and mindfulness.

A native Texan and horse-ranch owner, Johnson offers a book of meditative practices that she's tested and used as a teacher and in her own personal meditation. The book begins by addressing any apprehensions the uninitiated reader may have about meditation in general, ego-study and other self-awareness topics. But instead of pointing out the flaws of society's fast-paced left-brain–dominant structures, Johnson suggests practical approaches that harness human nature instead of denying it. For example, she suggests that instead of trying to dismiss their egos, readers should learn to embrace them as internal protection mechanisms. Only when you understand the true value of the ego, Johnson suggests, can you begin to live a life of harmony. She explains that people's thoughts don't need to be the dominant forces that control their feelings, and learning to control one's thoughts can help a person begin to explore the self, the body and the tangible world. Johnson compellingly presents meditation as a private process of learning about oneself, with no "correct" way to do it. She recommends trying out different visual, sonic and sensory styles of meditation until something fits. Overall, the book portrays meditation as the process of understanding how one functions. It's a framing that makes sense and contrasts with the ample time that many people spend deciphering how external entities work, from corporations to governments to technology. This self-discovery process may help readers better manage their thoughts and emotions and lead to the calmer, happier existence Johnson encourages.

A well-illustrated, concise guide to meditation.

—*Kirkus Reviews*

CPSIA information can be obtained at www.ICGtesting.com
Printed in the USA
LVOW061459190413

330033LV00001B/83/P